I0225579

JEWISH SWEETS

ALSO BY KENDEN ALFOND

Feeding Women of the Talmud, Feeding Ourselves: Uplifting the Voices of Talmudic Heroines and Honoring Them with Simple, Vegan Recipes

Beyond Chopped Liver: 59 Jewish Recipes Get a Vegan Health Makeover

Feeding Women of the Bible, Feeding Ourselves: Uplifting the Voices of Hebrew Biblical Heroines and Honoring Them with Simple Plant-Based Recipes

The Jewish Food Hero Cookbook: 50 Simple Plant-Based Recipes for Your Holiday Meals

JEWISH FOOD HERO

Nourishing your mind, body, and spirit

JEWISH SWEETS

A Worldwide Community Cookbook of 100 Dessert Recipes

Kenden Alfond

Author of *The Jewish Food Hero Cookbook*

TURNER
PUBLISHING COMPANY

Turner Publishing Company
Nashville, Tennessee
www.turnerpublishing.com

T

Copyright © 2025 by Kenden Alfond
Jewish Sweets: A Worldwide Community Cookbook of 100 Dessert Recipes

No part of this publication may be reproduced, stored in a retrieval system, or transmitted in any form or by any means, electronic, mechanical, photocopying, recording, scanning, or otherwise, except as permitted under Sections 107 or 108 of the 1976 United States Copyright Act, without either the prior written permission of the Publisher, or authorization through payment of the appropriate per-copy fee to the Copyright Clearance Center, 222 Rosewood Drive, Danvers, MA 01923, (978) 750-8400, fax (978) 750-4744. Requests to the Publisher for permission should be addressed to Turner Publishing Company, 4507 Charlotte Avenue, Suite 100, Nashville, Tennessee, 37209, (615) 255-2665, fax (615) 255-5081, E-mail: admin@turnerpublishing.com.

Limit of Liability/Disclaimer of Warranty: While the publisher and the author have used their best efforts in preparing this book, they make no representations or warranties with respect to the accuracy or completeness of the contents of this book and specifically disclaim any implied warranties of merchantability or fitness for a particular purpose. No warranty may be created or extended by sales representatives or written sales materials. The advice and strategies contained herein may not be suitable for your situation. You should consult with a professional where appropriate. Neither the publisher nor the author shall be liable for any loss of profit or any other commercial damages, including but not limited to special, incidental, consequential, or other damages.

Cover design: William Ruoto
Book design: Jena Hippensteel Henderson

Library of Congress Cataloging-in-Publication Data
Names: Alfond, Kenden, author.
Title: Jewish sweets : a worldwide community cookbook of 99 dessert recipes
  / Kenden Alfond.
Description: Nashville, Tennessee : Turner Publishing Company, 2025 |
  Includes index.
Identifiers: LCCN 2024011476 (print) | LCCN 2024011477 (ebook) | ISBN
  9798887980072 (hardcover) | ISBN 9798887980065 (paperback) | ISBN
  9798887980089 (epub)
Subjects: LCSH: Desserts. | Jewish cooking. | LCGFT: Cookbooks.
Classification: LCC TX773 .A348 2025 (print) | LCC TX773 (ebook) | DDC
  641.86--dc23/eng/20240410
LC record available at https://lccn.loc.gov/2024011476
LC ebook record available at https://lccn.loc.gov/2024011477

Printed in the United States of America

1 2 3 4 5 6 7 8 9 10

Only A Book

Our people embarked on a long journey
and in their hands, only a book.

Some peoples traveled
with only gold and silver,
with diamonds and jewels:
We, with this Book.

Some peoples have traveled
only with sword and armor,
with trumpets and flags,
with swords and shields:
We, with this Book.

Some peoples never traveled,
They stayed home,
rooted in their land,
blossoming in isolation,
and then decaying:
We journeyed, with this Book.

This is the Book
for which Israel was chosen,
The Book that places
people above beasts,

That made G-d's glory
the human life.

One G-d, One humanity,
One World.
This is the Book that gave
human dignity its origin,
social security its birth:
And to the humbly born
and the cruelly treated,
their claim to justice and to care.

Our people embarked
on a long journey,
and in their hands, only a Book;
Thanks to this Book,
Am Yisrael Chai, we live.

— Author Unknown, 1960

* Tom Cohen and Isa N. Konvitz (2020) Siddour Sefat Halev: Le Langage du Coeur/ The Language of the Heart

TABLE OF CONTENTS

INTRODUCTION

Jewish people have been writing down and sharing recipes since forever. Jewish cookbooks first and foremost are tied to Judaism and Jewish culture.

In this community cookbook, you will read dessert recipes, the stories behind them, lists of ingredients, and step-by-step instructions. And with your heart, you will walk into real and imagined Jewish kitchens around the world and feel a deep sense of being at "home." The kitchen is the heart of our home and is bound up with a deep sense of love, comfort, nourishment, togetherness, and memory.

The recipes in this book, in their totality, give us a real-time snapshot of the sweet treats that Jewish people are making today to honor our holidays and bring pleasure into everyday life.

COMMUNITY COOKBOOK

Jewish Sweets: A Worldwide Community Cookbook of 100 Dessert Recipes is a compilation of 100 recipes contributed by Jewish bakers and dessert makers from around the world. Their recipes invite us into the heart of family food stories, some of them stretching back through several generations and across continents.

Jewish community cookbooks are hidden gems in the world of Jewish food. They're a peek into the delicious and diverse food traditions of Jewish communities all over the globe. Community cookbooks document (and are) Jewish culture, passing down recipes from one generation to the next.

The application of the community cookbook format in a Jewish context carries a historic and geographic dimension. The migratory nature of the Jewish people, compelled by persecution and expulsion, has resulted in the worldwide dispersion of Jewish communities. When people migrate, whether by choice or as a necessity of survival, they take their recipes with them. With the exception of modern Israel, Jews have lived as minorities within other cultures. Jewish cuisine has evolved in response to the geographic and cultural contexts in which Jews found themselves.

HOW RECIPES REFLECT OUR COMMUNITY

CULTURAL DIVERSITY: In this book, there are recipes from Jews who were born, lived or grew up in, fled from or to, and settled in countries including: Argentina, Australia, Brazil, Cuba, Czech Republic, Egypt, Ethiopia, France, Germany, Hong Kong, India, Indonesia, Israel, Japan, Morocco, Poland, Russia, Singapore, Syria, Taiwan, Turkey, Ukraine, the United Kingdom, the United States, Uzbekistan, and beyond.

HISTORY AND MEMORY: Jewish recipes are not just about food. Many of the recipes in this book include family stories and historical context. History and memory are essential ingredients in the recipes that Jewish people share.

KOSHER DIETARY LAWS: Kosher laws instruct us that meat and milk are not to be eaten together, and that certain foods are completely forbidden, or forbidden during certain times of the year. This cookbook offers sweet recipes organized by categories: dairy, pareve, and kosher for Passover. This makes it easy to find the perfect dessert recipe to match with all our meals.

HOLIDAY RECIPES: *Jewish Sweets* offers dessert recipes to suit the special food traditions of Rosh Hashanah, Yom Kippur, Hanukkah, Purim, Passover, and Shavuot.

CLASSIC RECIPES: You'll see classics and updates of Jewish dessert recipes that are enduring favorites from the Ashkenazi, Sephardi, Mizrahi, and Bene Israel communities.

FUSION AND INNOVATION: Throughout history, Jewish communities have often lived as minorities within diverse cultures, fostering cultural exchange and culinary fusion. This dynamic has given rise to fusion recipes that blend traditional Jewish culinary traditions with local influences. Furthermore, converts to Judaism introduce their own culinary heritage and family recipes, contributing to the diversity and innovation within Jewish cuisine. Today, intermarriage is increasingly common within our community, further enriching Jewish food with a wider array of culinary influences.

CULINARY INFLUENCES WITHIN NATIONAL BORDERS: Jews adapt and adopt food behaviors and preferences in response to the geographic and cultural contexts in which they find themselves. Some of the recipes in this collection exemplify this phenomenon: a Jewish

American's favorite dessert recipe includes peanut butter, a Jewish Australian shares a pavlova recipe, and a British Jew shares a chocolate pudding recipe (not to be confused with American pudding).

HEALTH TRENDS: Modern food trends impact everyone, including Jews! There is a demand for healthier desserts, vegan and plant-based options, adaptations and options that are gluten-free, macro-friendly, keto, lower sugar, or portion-controlled miniature-sized desserts. This book includes several recipes that embrace up-to-date nutritional guidance.

In short, Jewish community cookbooks aren't just about cooking—they're like a tasty time capsule. Community cookbooks keep traditional recipes alive and introduce new recipes into Jewish food culture.

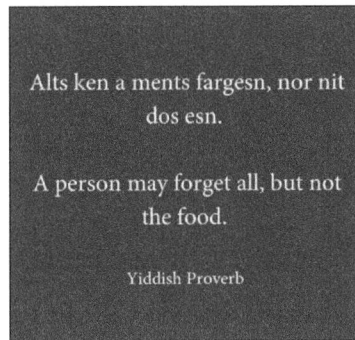

Alts ken a ments fargesn, nor nit dos esn.

A person may forget all, but not the food.

Yiddish Proverb

JEWISH FOOD AND DESSERT RECIPES

This book takes a broad interpretation of "Jewish food," encompassing both quintessential Jewish classics and whatever desserts Jews are eating today.

The choice to share the unique recipes in this book is not a statement that these recipes belong to the Jewish community exclusively, or that they originated in the Jewish community—far from it, in fact. Some foods are commonly eaten by Jews but have their origins in other cultures. Other recipes created by Jews have been and are eaten by non-Jews as well.

Whereas recipes used to be passed from person to person via paper and the handwritten note, the unfolding of the digital media age in the second half of the 20th century, and the current ubiquity of internet access, television, and social media use have all significantly increased people's access to other food cultures and recipes.

OUR HEALTH

It might seem paradoxical to talk about healthy eating in the introduction to a dessert cookbook. Bear with me!

Global diets have changed in recent decades. There has been an increase in the consumption of foods that are high in fats and sugars. Today, obesity and pre-obesity (i.e., being overweight) in children, adolescents, and adults is a public health concern in almost all regions of the world. It's important to recognize that weight gain and obesity are complex issues influenced by a combination of genetic, environmental, and lifestyle factors. Most of us live in obesogenic environments where there are physical, economic, political, social, and cultural factors that promote obesity and overeating. For example, living in a place where ultra-processed foods are cheap and readily available, where snacking and overeating are normalized, and where there is a decrease in physical activity due to the changing nature of many types of work, more access to passive forms of transportation, and increased urbanization. There are multiple dietary fads which respond to this culture of excess by promoting the restriction or exclusion of entire food groups. Extremes of food consumption or food restriction are equally damaging.

Enjoying all food in moderation, including desserts, is essential for our emotional well-being because it gives us pleasure. In this food context, we need to find straightforward, practical ways of thinking about food and eating that honor our desires to enjoy all food, all the while achieving and maintaining our physical health. One balance point is portion control.

HAVING OUR CAKE AND EATING IT, TOO

It's possible to enjoy all foods, including desserts. A simple key is portion control.

PORTION CONTROL:
Managing the quantity or size of the foods consumed during a meal or snack.
Portion control is an essential aspect of maintaining a healthy diet
and managing body weight.

Here is how practicing portion control can support us:

- **CALORIC INTAKE:** Portion size directly affects caloric intake. Consuming too many calories regularly can lead to weight gain and obesity, associated with various physical health problems and mental health consequences.

- **NUTRIENT BALANCE:** Proper portion control helps ensure a balanced intake of essential nutrients. When you control portion sizes, you are more likely to consume the appropriate proportions of carbohydrates, proteins, and fats, as well as vitamins and minerals, necessary for overall health.

- **BLOOD SUGAR REGULATION:** Overconsumption, especially of foods high in sugars and refined carbohydrates, can lead to spikes in blood sugar levels. Appropriate portion sizes help stabilize blood sugar levels.

- **DIGESTIVE HEALTH:** Eating large portions can strain the digestive system and lead to discomfort, bloating, and indigestion. Smaller, well-portioned meals can support better digestion and absorption of nutrients.

- **HUNGER AND FULLNESS SIGNALS:** Listening to your body's hunger and fullness signals is crucial for maintaining a healthy weight. Overeating can disrupt these signals, making it harder to recognize genuine hunger and satisfaction.

- **WEIGHT MANAGEMENT:** Portion control is a fundamental aspect of weight management. It helps create a calorie deficit for weight loss, a balance for weight maintenance, or excess for weight gain. By consuming appropriate portions, you are more likely to achieve and maintain a healthy weight.

- **MINDFUL EATING:** Being aware of portion sizes promotes mindful eating. This means paying attention to what you eat, savoring your food, and enjoying the eating experience. Mindful eating can help prevent distracted overconsumption and improve your relationship with food.

- **PREVENTING OVERINDULGENCE:** Large portions can encourage overeating, as we tend to eat whatever is on the plate, ignoring our satiety signals. Portion control can help prevent this overindulgence.

- **LONG-TERM HABITS:** Developing a habit of controlling portion sizes is a key component of maintaining a healthy lifestyle. It encourages mindful eating and makes it easier to sustain a balanced diet over the long term.

You might think skipping the fun foods and treats is "healthier," but the opposite tends to be true. Banning any food with the intention of eliminating it usually intensifies the desire for it, triggering food cravings and overconsumption. On the other hand, eating a moderate amount of fun foods and treats is psychologically beneficial, as it provokes pleasure and increases self-trust around food. Eating a reasonably sized delicious dessert is suddenly not a crisis or mistake, it is just a pleasing moment.

Today, health to me means eating everything, in balance. This includes enjoying appropriately portioned sweet treats on a daily basis. Most people find that they feel at their physical and mental/ emotional best spending 80–90% of their daily calories on minimally processed whole foods like fruits, vegetables, high-quality proteins, nuts, seeds, starches, and whole grains. The remaining 10–20% of the daily calorie budget can be spent on fun foods and treats, however you define them.

ABOUT THE MEASUREMENTS: METRIC AND IMPERIAL

This community cookbook features dessert recipes from contributors worldwide. To preserve authenticity and accuracy, these recipes have been edited for clarity only, maintaining each contributor's original measuring systems. You will need to be equipped with a kitchen scale to make the recipes which use metric measurements and measuring cups for those recipes with ingredients listed in imperial measurements.

CHARITY

All of the contributors, including me, volunteered their time and intellectual energy to create this book. As such, all Jewish Food Hero's profits from the sale of this book will be donated to Jewish nonprofits.

A FINAL NOTE

I am completing this community cookbook in January 2024. This is a profoundly challenging period, marked by the tragic terror attacks in Israel on October 7, 2023, and a troubling surge of antisemitism worldwide. While I acknowledge that recipes alone cannot transform the global political landscape toward justice and truth, nor can they single-handedly awaken people to the perils and irrationality of antisemitism, I still firmly believe in the value of food as a means of fostering connection among people. Through the act of reading recipe stories and preparing nourishing dishes for our loved ones, we can find moments of pleasure and unity.

My aspiration is that this cookbook will serve as a bridge connecting you to our global Jewish community. I hope that as you read its pages and prepare the heartfelt recipes within, it will feel like kindling a candle of hope, offering a sense of togetherness during these challenging times.

I am so glad you are here. To our health and inspiration.

Am Yisrael Chai!

DAIRY RECIPES

ALFAJORES: SANDWICH COOKIES WITH DULCE DE LECHE FILLING

Contributed by Marina Shamesh

PREP TIME: 30 minutes | **COOK TIME:** 10–15 minutes
TOTAL TIME: 2 hours including dough resting time | **YIELD:** 20 cookies

Israel is a melting pot of people from all over the world who come with their own culture, opinions, and sense of style, but—most importantly!—immigrants bring their food. The Alfajores cookie illustrates this point. This shortbread type of sandwich cookie, filled with caramel and rolled in coconut, is often found in bakeries and coffee shops here in Israel. I was enchanted by these staple "Israeli" cookies the first time I saw them. Later I learned that the Alfajores cookies came to Israel with the Argentinian immigrants. Making these cookies takes a bit of work, though not *that* much. They look and taste amazing and are worth the effort!

Ingredients:

- 100 grams soft butter
- ¾ cup granulated sugar
- 1 large egg
- 1 teaspoon grated lemon zest
- 150 grams cornflour
- ½ cup flour
- 1 teaspoon baking powder
- 1 cup caramel or dulce de leche
- 50 grams shredded coconut

Tools:

- Baking sheets
- Cling wrap
- Cookie cutter or cup
- Kitchen scale
- Measuring cups and spoons
- Medium mixing bowl
- Rolling pin
- Spoon
- Stand mixer or mixing bowl and wooden spoon
- Zester or fine grater

Instructions:

1. Mix the butter and sugar in a mixer or medium mixing bowl. Add the egg and continue to mix well.
2. Add the lemon zest, cornflour, flour, and baking powder. Mix until the dough is smooth.
3. Cover the dough in cling film and set aside for one hour in the fridge.
4. Heat the oven to 170°C / 340°F.
5. Divide the dough into three. On a floured surface, roll out one third to a thickness of about half a centimeter.
6. Use a round cookie cutter or upturned cup to cut out circles from the rolled-out dough and place them on baking sheets.
7. Bake until golden, about 15 minutes.
8. Repeat with the rest of the dough and leave the cookies to cool.
9. Use a spoon to spread a bit of the caramel between and on the outer edge of two cookies sandwiched together.
10. Roll in coconut and there you have it—a delicious Alfajores cookie.
11. Serve with coffee or a pot of tea and remember to save some for your guests!

MARINA SHAMESH was born in South Africa and has lived in Israel since 1996, in the picturesque town of Zichron Yaakov. She loves to write, take photographs, and create generative art. Her understanding of the world is that doing something creative is as important as breathing. During work hours, Marina is a project manager.

APPLES AND HONEY BOURBON BREAD PUDDING

Contributed by Beth Kander

PREP TIME: 20 minutes | **COOK TIME:** 35–40 minutes
TOTAL TIME: 1 hour | **YIELD:** 10+ servings

I've often joked that in my family, some folks are Jewish, some are Southern—and I'm the first one who got to be both. I moved to Jackson, Mississippi, right after college and lived there for more than a decade. (I even wound up marrying a nice New Orleans boy!) Steeped in southern and Jewish culture, I played around with the flavors from all the incredible cultural influences in my life. One of my favorite creations is my Apples and Honey Bourbon Bread Pudding. The recipe has become my Rosh Hashanah tradition: a Southern-and-Jewish recipe that celebrates the season, blending a particular tradition with a particular geography. It's meaningful, delicious, and tells a story with every bite.

Ingredients:

For the bread pudding:
- 10 cups of challah chunks (approximately one big loaf, torn)
- 1 can (12 ounces) evaporated milk
- 1 cup (240 grams) milk
- 1 cup (240 grams) half-and-half
- 5 eggs, beaten
- ½ cup (100 grams) granulated sugar
- ½ cup (170 grams) honey
- ½ cup (113 grams) butter
- 1 teaspoon vanilla extract
- 1 teaspoon cinnamon

- 2 teaspoons baking powder
- Dash of salt
- 2 cups (236 grams) peeled and chopped apple

For the sauce:
- ½ packed cup (110 grams) brown sugar
- ½ cup (170 grams) light corn syrup
- ½ cup (113 grams) butter
- ¼ cup (32 grams) honey bourbon (optional)

BETH KANDER is a writer with tangled roots in the Midwest and Deep South. She has an MSW from the University of Michigan and an MFA from Mississippi University for Women. Beth enjoys travel and stay-cations equally. Food is one of her many love languages; meals are terrific settings for storytelling. Her favorite characters are her two brave, hilarious kids.

Tools:

- Baking dish, 9" x 13"
- Chopping board
- Kitchen scale
- Large mixing bowl
- Measuring cups and spoons
- Sharp knife
- Small saucepan
- Whisk
- Wooden spoon or rubber spatula

Instructions:

Make the pudding:

1. Preheat the oven to 350°F.
2. Lightly grease a 9" x 13" baking dish.
3. Place the torn challah pieces in the baking dish.
4. In a large bowl, mix evaporated milk, milk, half-and-half, eggs, sugar, honey, butter, vanilla, cinnamon, baking powder, and salt. Thoroughly combine, then pour the mixture over the challah chunks.
5. Let it sit for about 10 minutes so the challah can absorb all the deliciousness.
6. Add the apples, mixing to distribute throughout the challah pieces.
7. Bake for approximately 30–40 minutes, until the pudding is a beautiful light golden color.
8. Remove from the oven and let cool for 5 minutes before topping with sauce.

Make the honey bourbon sauce:

9. Make the sauce while the bread pudding is cooling—it's a quick process! Combine sugar, corn syrup, and butter in a small saucepan over medium heat.
10. Bring to a simmer; cook for about a minute, stirring it constantly.
11. Remove from heat and stir in the honey bourbon. (This is optional and can be skipped if you're avoiding alcohol, but the very small amount adds a nice richness to the flavor.)

Serve:

12. Immediately drizzle one tablespoon of sauce over each serving of bread pudding. Serve warm and enjoy.

APPLE-LEMON CAKE

Contributed by Julia Kogan

PREP TIME: 1 hour | **COOK TIME:** 30 minutes
TOTAL TIME: 1 hour 30 minutes | **YIELD:** 1 kilo of cake, serves 10–12 people

Russian dessert cuisine features an infinite variety of apple cakes and pies because in many cases apples were the only fruit available. This particular cake is a tribute to my childhood memories of grandma's apple cake. We always had it for tea, and the tea was always taken, of course, with lemon. Here, lemon adds a hint of sourness to balance the sweetness of the apple, and walnuts add a necessary crunch!

Ingredients:

For the biscuit:
- 50 grams egg yolk
- 50 grams honey
- Zest of one lemon
- 100 grams almond flour
- 30 grams wheat flour
- 50 grams 82% butter
- 100 grams egg white
- 100 grams sugar

For the walnut crunch:
- 25 grams white chocolate
- 25 grams walnut paste
- 35 grams waffle crumb

For the apple compote:
- 2 grams gelatin
- 10 grams ice water (for soaking gelatin)

- 130 grams diced apple (0.8 x 0.8cm cubes)
- 60 grams sugar, halved
- 5 grams pectin
- 50 grams lemon puree (or juice)
- 90 grams water
- 40 grams honey

For the lemon cream:
- 5 grams gelatin
- 35 grams ice water (for soaking gelatin)
- 75 grams whole egg
- 75 grams egg yolk
- 100 grams sugar
- 100 grams lemon puree (or juice)
- 100 grams 82% butter, chopped

Tools:

- Bain-marie or saucepan
- Cooking thermometer
- Cutting board
- Glass mixing bowl
- Kitchen scale
- Measuring cups and spoons
- Medium mixing bowls
- Saucepans
- Sharp knife
- Side tape (optional)

- Silicone mat
- Small prep bowls x 4
- Spatula
- Square metal tin or silicone mold for assembly (16 x 16 x 5cm)
- Stick blender or food processor
- Whisk
- Zester
- *A good mood*

Instructions:

Make the biscuit:

1. Preheat the oven to 170°C / 340°F.
2. Combine yolks, honey, and zest in a medium mixing bowl with a whisk. Mix both flours together in a medium mixing bowl, then add to the yolk mixture along with the melted butter. Stir with spatula to combine.
3. In a separate medium bowl, whisk the egg whites and sugar until they form peaks. Gently fold egg white mixture into the other ingredients, adding a bit at a time. Spread the biscuit mixture onto a silicone mat, it should be about 1cm thick. Bake for approximately 25 minutes.
4. Allow the biscuit to cool before cutting into three 16 x 16cm squares.

Make the walnut crunch:

5. In a medium bowl, melt the chocolate and mix in the remaining ingredients. Pour into the square tin or silicone mold and freeze.

Make the apple compote:

6. Soak the gelatin in ice water.
7. Place the cubed apple with half of the sugar in a saucepan over medium heat. Bring to a boil and simmer until soft.
8. Mix the remaining half of the sugar with pectin in a small bowl and set aside.

9. In another saucepan, combine the lemon puree (or juice) with water and honey. Heat until the honey dissolves, but don't allow the temperature to exceed 40°C (104°F).

10. Sprinkle the pectin and sugar mixture into the lemon honey pan, add the softened gelatin and apple mixture, and stir to combine thoroughly and then turn off the heat.

Make the lemon cream:

11. Soak the gelatin in ice water and set aside.

12. Add the egg, yolk, sugar, and lemon puree (or juice) to a glass bowl and whisk to combine.

13. Set the glass bowl over a bain-marie and bring the mixture to 82°C, whisking constantly and vigorously.

14. Add the softened gelatin and whisk to combine.

15. Allow the mix to cool to 35–40°C, then add the chopped butter. Using a stick blender or food processor, blend until smooth and homogenous and then turn off the heat.

Assemble the layers:

16. Place one of the biscuit squares into the bottom of the square tin or silicone mold.

17. Top with ⅓ of the lemon cream, spread evenly.

18. Add the crunchy walnut layer.

19. Add another ⅓ of the lemon cream.

20. Place the second biscuit layer into the mold, then top with the apple compote.

21. Finally, add the final biscuit layer and top with the remaining lemon cream.

JULIA KOGAN is the founder, owner, and head pastry chef of Conditoria school and patisserie in Ekaterinburg, Russia. Her cakes and desserts combine exotic local ingredients, such as bird cherry and cowberry, with modern pastry techniques.

APRICOT, CINNAMON, AND WALNUT RUGELACH

Contributed by Rose Levy Beranbaum

PREP TIME: 1 hour 30 minutes, plus 30 minutes chilling time or overnight
COOK TIME: 15–20 minutes | **TOTAL TIME:** 1 hour 50 minutes, plus chilling time
YIELD: 24 2½-inch cookies

If there could be just one sweet treat in the world, I would choose a dairy rugelach for the flavor and texture. Did I grow up with Rugelach? No. My mother was a dentist, and sweets were seldom in the house. The cinnamon-imbued dough is comfortingly soft, yet crisp. The sticky tang of caramelized apricot, juicy plump chewiness of raisins, and earthy crunch of walnuts, all rolled into each and every bite: utterly irresistible. I first published this recipe in the book *Rose's Christmas Cookies* (1990), and it has since been republished in *The Baking Bible* (2014), *Rose's Baking Basics* (2018), and *The Cookie Bible* (2022).

Ingredients:

For the dough:
- 1 cup lightly spooned and leveled off plus 2½ tablespoons (145 grams) bleached all-purpose flour
- ⅛ teaspoon fine sea salt
- ½ cup minus 1 tablespoon (64 grams) cream cheese
- 6 tablespoons (¾ stick / 85 grams) unsalted butter, at 65-75°F (19-23°C)
- 2 tablespoons (25 grams) granulated sugar
- ½ teaspoon (2.5 milliliters) pure vanilla extract

For the filling:
- 3 tablespoons (37 grams) granulated sugar

- 2 tablespoons firmly packed (27 grams) light brown Muscovado sugar or dark brown sugar
- ¼ teaspoon ground cinnamon
- ¼ cup plus 2 tablespoons (54 grams) golden raisins
- ½ cup (50 grams) walnuts, coarsely chopped
- ¼ cup (76 grams) Apricot Lekvar Filling or apricot preserve

For the topping:
- 1 tablespoon (13 grams) granulated sugar
- ½ teaspoon ground cinnamon
- 1 tablespoon milk

Tools:

- Cookie sheets x 2, 15" x 12", lined with foil
- Food processor or handheld mixer
- Kitchen scale
- Knife
- Measuring cups and spoons
- Pastry brush
- Pizza wheel or long sharp knife
- Plastic wrap

- Prep bowls
- Rolling pin
- Small pancake turner (spatula)
- Small spatula or tablespoon
- Spatula
- Whisk
- Wire cooling racks x 2, lightly coated with nonstick cooking spray

Instructions:

Make the dough:

1. In a small bowl, whisk together the flour and salt.
2. Combine the remaining ingredients, then add the flour, using one of the following methods:
   Handheld mixer method: In a medium mixing bowl on medium speed, beat the cream cheese and butter until blended. Beat in the sugar and vanilla. On low speed, beat in the flour mixture just until incorporated, no more than 30 seconds.
   Food processor method: Have the cream cheese and butter chilled. Cut the butter into ½-inch cubes. Place the cream cheese in a food processor. With the motor running, add the butter and process until smooth and creamy, scraping down the sides of the bowl once or twice, using a spatula. Add the sugar and vanilla and process for a few seconds to incorporate them. Add the flour mixture and pulse in just until the dough starts to clump together.
3. Scrape the dough onto a piece of plastic wrap, using a spatula, and press it together to form a ball. Divide the dough in half, about 6.5 ounces / 185 grams each. Wrap each piece loosely in plastic wrap and press to form flat discs. Rewrap tightly and refrigerate for a minimum of 1 hour or up to 3 days (or freeze for up to 6 months).

Make the filling:

4. In a medium bowl, with your fingers, mix the granulated sugar, brown sugar, and cinnamon until evenly combined. Divide the mixture equally between two small bowls.

5. Combine the golden raisins and the chopped walnuts and divide them equally between two additional small bowls. Note: If the raisins are not soft, first soak them in ½ cup (118 milliliters) boiling water for 30 minutes to 1 hour and then drain them well.

Roll the dough:

6. Remove one half of the dough from the refrigerator and let it sit on the counter for about 5 to 10 minutes, or until it is malleable enough to roll.

7. Using a floured rolling pin on a lightly floured surface, roll out the dough into about a 9-inch circle, ⅛-inch thick, rotating it often and adding flour as necessary to be sure it is not sticking. If the dough becomes too soft or sticky at any time, briefly refrigerate it until it is firm enough to roll.

Add the filling:

8. Mark the center of the dough with the tip of a knife. Using the back of a tablespoon or small offset spatula, spread the dough evenly with 2 tablespoons (30 milliliters) of the apricot lekvar, avoiding about 1 inch in the center because the filling will push forward when shaping. If using preserve, stir with a fork to break up any large pieces, but do not heat or beat because it will thin.

9. Sprinkle half of the sugar mixture over the lekvar. Sprinkle evenly with half of the raisin and walnut mixture. Press the filling gently but firmly over the dough.

10. Slip a large spatula under the dough disc to loosen it from the work surface. Using a pizza wheel or long sharp knife, cut the dough into 12 triangles: first cut the dough into quarters, and then cut each quarter into thirds.

Shape the Rugelach:

11. Use a thin knife or spatula, if necessary, to loosen the triangles from the work surface. Starting at the wide end, roll up the triangle and bend the ends around to form a slight crescent shape, turning them toward the point. Place the rugelach, point underneath, about 1½ inches apart on a prepared cookie sheet.

Add the topping:

12. In a small bowl, stir together the sugar and cinnamon for the topping. Divide the mixture equally between two small bowls.

13. Lift each rugelach with your fingers and brush it with milk. Holding the rugelach over a medium bowl, use your fingers to sprinkle the rugelach evenly with the cinnamon sugar, letting the excess fall into the bowl. Set the rugelach back on the cookie sheet.

14. Cover the cookie sheet with plastic wrap and refrigerate the rugelach for at least 30 minutes or up to overnight, until firm.

15. Repeat with the second disc of dough.

Bake the Rugelach:

16. Twenty minutes or longer before baking, set oven racks in the upper and lower thirds of the oven and preheat the oven to 350°F / 175°C.

17. Bake for 10 minutes. For even baking, rotate the cookie sheets halfway around and reverse their positions from top to bottom. Continue baking for 5-10 minutes, or until lightly browned.

18. Remove the cookie sheets from the oven and place on uncoated wire racks or a heat-proof surface, and let the rugelach cool for a few minutes to firm slightly. During baking, a little of the apricot always melts out onto the foil. It is therefore necessary to remove the rugelach from the foil before the apricot hardens. Use a small pancake turner to transfer the rugelach to the prepared wire racks to cool completely. The apricot filling that leaks onto the foil liner can be peeled off and makes for a delicious baker's treat!

19. Store in an airtight container at room temperature for 5 days, or frozen for 3 months.

ROSE LEVY BERANBAUM is an American baker, cookbook author, and food writer. Rose has published thirteen books including *Romantic & Classic Cakes* (1981), *The Cake Bible* (1988), *The Baking Bible* (2014), *Rose's Baking Basics* (2018), *Rose's Ice Cream Bliss* (2020), and *The Cookie Bible* (2022). Rose is a three-time James Beard Award winner.

BANANA BREAD: CHOCK FULL OF GOODIES

Contributed by Laura Kumin

PREP TIME: 20 minutes | **COOK TIME:** 1 hour 30 minutes
TOTAL TIME: 1 hour 50 minutes | **YIELD:** 8–10 servings

An easy and delicious breakfast or snack, this banana bread is moist and filled with chips, nuts, granola, and/or raisins. This banana bread, adapted from my friend's recipe, was one of the first things I ever baked that didn't come from a boxed mix. Still one of my all-time favorites, I've tweaked the recipe slightly over the years, but remain true to the basics of the original version. I still have the now-battered black notebook where I first wrote it down. The page for this recipe got stained and the ink smeared in places; it's still readable though—and that's all that matters.

Ingredients:

- 1 cup all-purpose white flour
- 1 teaspoon baking soda
- ½ teaspoon kosher or fine sea salt
- 1 cup brown or white whole wheat flour
- ½ cup (¼ pound or 1 stick) unsalted butter
- 1 cup sugar
- 3 medium extra ripe bananas, mashed
- 2 eggs at room temperature
- ⅓ cup hot water (heated in microwave or on stove until simmering)
- ½–1 cup add-ins (I use ½ cup chocolate chips and ½ cup chopped nuts, but you can also add granola and/or raisins)

Tools:

- Baking spray (optional)
- Cast iron loaf pan
- Fork
- Kitchen scale
- Measuring cups and spoons
- Medium saucepan (optional)
- Prep bowls
- Spatula
- Whisk
- Wire rack
- Wooden mixing spoon

LAURA KUMIN is an author, teacher, and cooking coach. Her books, *All Stirred Up: Suffrage Cookbooks, Food, and the Battle for Women's Right to Vote* and *The Hamilton Cookbook: Cooking, Eating & Entertaining in Hamilton's World* combine history, culture, and cooking. Laura writes on her blog, motherwouldknow.com, and for major publications. She often presents on podcasts and cooking programs.

Instructions:

1. Preheat the oven to 325°F.
2. Generously butter a heavy loaf pan and coat it with flour by adding a spoonful of flour to the pan and shifting the pan around until it is coated with flour. Set aside. Alternatively, coat the pan with a baking spray that combines neutral or butter-flavored oil with flour. Discard any remaining flour.
3. In a small bowl, whisk together the white flour, baking soda, and salt. Add the whole wheat or white whole wheat flour and whisk again until the two flours are well combined. Set aside.
4. Melt the butter in the microwave in a medium-large microwavable bowl or on the stovetop in a similar sized pot. Add the sugar and mix until combined.
5. In a medium bowl, combine the mashed bananas and the eggs. Mix them until the eggs are mixed in but the bananas remain lumpy. Pour the mixture into the butter and sugar and stir until combined.
6. Alternate adding the dry ingredients and the hot water to the batter in about 3–4 batches, beginning with the dry ingredients. Stir after each addition. Once the mixture is fully combined, add in the chocolate chips, nuts, granola, and/or raisins.
7. Pour the mixture into the loaf pan and bake for 70–90 minutes or until a long skewer comes out clean.
8. Cool the loaf completely in the pan on a wire rack. Once it is completely cool, run a knife around the edges and unmold the loaf.

RECIPE NOTES:

*   I put a large sheet pan on the shelf below the loaf pan to catch any drips, so they don't burn on the bottom of the oven. Typically it is not necessary; the loaf simply rises with a nice "bump" in the middle and there are no drips. But it's better to be safe than sorry. Do not put the sheet pan on the same shelf as the loaf pan as that alters the baking time.
*   If you check the banana bread and the top is browned before the center is fully baked, put a piece of foil loosely on the top as it continues to bake until the center is firm.
*   This recipe also works perfectly for banana bread muffins.

BASBOUSA BIL ZABADI: SEMOLINA CAKE WITH YOGURT

Contributed by Viviane Bowell

PREP TIME: 20 minutes | **COOK TIME:** 50–60 minutes
TOTAL TIME: 1 hour 10–20 minutes | **YIELD:** 24 pieces

Basbousa is a cake traditionally served with tea or coffee in Egypt. It is one of the many Egyptian cakes which relies on a final coating of cooled sugar syrup to soften and sweeten it. There are many ways of making basbousa, the most popular being with yogurt and coconut or almonds. I have used a mixture of yogurt and coconut in this recipe.

Ingredients:

For the syrup:
- 400 grams sugar
- 2 cups (500 milliliters) water
- Juice of half a lemon
- 3–4 drops vanilla essence

For the basbousa:
- 125 grams fine semolina
- 100 grams coarse semolina
- 25 grams desiccated coconut, mixed with 2 tablespoons of milk
- 225 grams sugar
- 150 milliliters full fat plain yogurt
- 1 teaspoon baking powder
- 125 grams unsalted butter, melted, plus extra for greasing

Tools:

- Cake pan, 15cm x 25cm (6" x 10")
- Kitchen scale
- Large mixing bowl
- Measuring cups and spoons
- Saucepan
- Sharp knife
- Spatula

Instructions:

1. Begin by making the syrup: combine the sugar, water and lemon juice in a pan. Bring to the boil then reduce the heat and simmer for 10 minutes until the syrup reduces and thickens. Add the vanilla and leave to cool. Place in the fridge until the basbousa is ready to come out of the oven.

2. Preheat the oven to 180°C / Gas Mark 4. Grease and line a 15cm x 25cm (6" x 10") cake pan.

3. Combine the two semolinas, the coconut mixture, sugar, yogurt, and baking powder in a large mixing bowl. Add the melted butter and mix thoroughly with a spatula.

4. Put the mixture in the cake pan and press firmly into place.

5. Place in the center of the oven for 50–60 minutes or until golden brown.

6. When cooked, remove the cake from the oven and cut into diamonds or squares. Immediately pour the cold syrup over the hot basbousa.

VIVIANE BOWELL was born and raised in a Jewish Sephardic community in Cairo, Egypt. In 1956, 14-year-old Viviane and her family were forced to leave as a result of the Suez crisis, and arrived in the UK as refugees. Viviane's book *To Egypt with Love* traces her childhood memories of the diverse customs and traditions she grew up surrounded by.

BLACK AND WHITE COOKIES

Contributed by Emily Paster

PREP TIME: 45 minutes | **COOK TIME:** 15 minutes
TOTAL TIME: 1 hour | **YIELD:** 16 Cookies

Glaser's Bake Shop on the Upper East Side, which was founded by Bavarian immigrants, invented the black and white cookie in the early part of the 20th century. (Sadly, Glaser's closed its doors in 2018 after 116 years.) The black and white cookie became strongly associated with Jewish bakeries in and around New York City. Today, the cookie remains popular, mostly on the East Coast, because of its soft, cakey texture, the hint of lemon (good) or almond (bad) and the signature half-chocolate, half-vanilla icing. Black and white cookies even made an appearance in an iconic episode of the '90s television show *Seinfeld*, ensuring their immortality.

Ingredients:

For the cookies:

- 2 cups all-purpose flour
- 1 teaspoon baking powder
- ½ teaspoon fine sea salt
- ¼ teaspoon baking soda
- 4 ounces unsalted butter at room temperature
- 1 cup granulated sugar
- Zest of one lemon
- 2 large eggs, room temperature
- 1 tablespoon vanilla extract
- 2 tablespoons milk
- ½ cup sour cream

For the icing:

- 2 ½ cups powdered sugar, sifted
- 7 tablespoons milk, divided
- 1 tablespoon corn syrup
- 1 teaspoon vanilla extract
- ¼ cup cocoa powder, sifted

Tools:

- Baking sheets x 2
- Kitchen scale
- Measuring cups and spoons
- Mixing bowls
- Parchment paper
- Sieve or sifter

- Spatula, regular and offset, or knife
- Stand mixer or handheld electric mixer
- Whisk
- Wire cooling rack
- Zester

Instructions:

---

1. Preheat the oven to 350°F and line two baking sheets with parchment paper.

2. Whisk together the flour, baking powder, salt, and baking soda in a small bowl. Set aside.

3. Cream the butter, sugar, and lemon zest in a stand mixer on medium-high speed until light and fluffy, about 5 minutes.

4. Add the eggs, vanilla, and milk and beat on medium-high speed until combined, about another minute. Scrape down the sides of the bowl with a spatula.

5. Alternate adding the dry ingredients and sour cream to the bowl, beginning and ending with the dry ingredients, mixing after each addition and scraping down the sides as necessary. Mix just until combined.

6. Measure out ¼ cup of batter and place it on the prepared cookie sheet. Repeat until you have four cookies per sheet. (Aim for 1.75–2 ounces of weight per cookie.) Spread each mound of batter in the shape of a circle until the batter is approximately ½-inch thick. Repeat with the second baking sheet.

7. Bake the cookies for 12–14 minutes, rotating the tray 180 degrees halfway through. Cool cookies on the sheet briefly then remove the cookies to a wire rack to cool. Repeat with the remaining batter. Allow the cookies to cool completely before attempting to ice them.

8. To make the icing, whisk together the powdered sugar, 4 tablespoons of milk, the corn syrup, and the vanilla in a medium bowl. The icing should be thick but spreadable.

9. Turn the cookies over so the flat side (or the bottom of the cookie) is facing up. This is the side you will glaze. Spread the white icing on one half of each cookie in a thin, even, opaque layer using a small offset spatula or knife. Place cookies on a wire rack, icing-side up, and allow the

icing to harden completely before proceeding with the chocolate icing. (Cover the bowl so the remaining icing does not dry out.)

10. Add the cocoa powder to the remaining white icing. Add 2 tablespoons of milk and whisk until the icing has reached a thick but spreadable texture. (If the mixture is not sweet enough to your liking, or you are running low after glazing the cookies with the white icing, add a ¼ cup more of powdered sugar and more milk if necessary.)

11. Glaze the second half of each cookie and allow the icing to harden completely before storing the cookies.

12. Cookies can be stored in an airtight container for up to 3 days.

EMILY PASTER is a lawyer turned food writer who focuses on globally inspired Jewish cuisine. She is the author of four cookbooks, including the best-selling *Epic Air Fryer*. Her latest book *Instantly Mediterranean: Vibrant Satisfying Recipes for Your Instant Pot, Electric Pressure Cooker & Air Fryer* was released in 2021. Emily lives outside Chicago with her husband and two ravenous teenagers.

BUBBE TAMARA'S POPPY SEED ROLL

Contributed by Valeria Asher

PREP TIME: 3 hours │ **COOK TIME:** 45 minutes
TOTAL TIME: 3 hours 45 minutes │ **YIELD:** 2 large rolls

The poppy seed roll is a quintessential Ukrainian dessert. This recipe is based on my memories of cooking with my bubbe Tamara. Making and eating this poppy seed roll brings me back to my childhood: a nice linen tablecloth, a tea set, and a beautiful plate with freshly baked poppy seed rolls in the middle of the table for all of us to share.

Ingredients:

For the filling:

- 2 cups poppy seeds
- ½ cup sugar
- 1 cup milk
- ¼ teaspoon salt
- ⅓ cup cold butter
- 1 teaspoon vanilla extract
- Zest of 1 lemon
- ½ cup walnuts
- ½ cup raisins
- ⅓ cup breadcrumbs
- 1 egg

For the dough:

- 1 teaspoon sugar
- 2 teaspoons yeast
- ½ cup warm water
- 3 ½ cups all-purpose flour
- ½ cup sugar
- ⅓ cup butter, room temperature
- 1 egg
- 1 teaspoon room-temperature milk

Tools:
_____

- Cheesecloth (or a clean kitchen towel)
- Food processor or coffee grinder or mortar and pestle (it must have a small enough blade or else the poppy seeds will just spin around without breaking up)
- Knife
- Measuring cups and spoons
- Mixing bowls
- Rolling pin
- Saucepan

Instructions:
_____

1. Grind poppy seeds using your preferred method and place in a prep bowl.
2. Cover the poppy seeds with 4 cups of freshly boiled water and let sit for 20 minutes.
3. Drain the poppy seeds into a cheesecloth, tying the opposing corners into knots, then hang it over a bowl or sink so that the remaining water drains completely. Leave hanging ideally overnight or for at least 1 hour.
4. Combine the poppy seeds with sugar, milk, and salt in a saucepan. Heat on low until it begins to thicken. Remove from heat.
5. Add cold butter, vanilla, and lemon zest.
6. In a food processor chop the raisins and walnuts. Add to the poppy seed mix.
7. Add the breadcrumbs and egg. Mix well.
8. Put the mixture in the refrigerator while you prepare the dough.

To make the dough:

9. Add 1 teaspoon of sugar and yeast to the warm water. Stir gently and set aside until it begins to bubble.
10. In a large mixing bowl, combine the flour and the remaining ½ cup of sugar.
11. Add ⅓ cup of room temperature butter and mix until well combined.
12. Add the yeast mixture and mix until a soft dough forms. Add the egg and mix well.
13. Cover and let the dough rise for 45 minutes.
14. Preheat the oven to 350°F / 180°C.
15. Cut the dough in half. Take the first half and roll it into a rectangle.

16. Spread half of the poppy seed mix on top of the rolled-out dough. Spread it evenly, leaving a little border. Roll the rectangle starting with the long side, and move it onto a baking sheet. Repeat with the second half of the dough.

17. Cover with cheesecloth or clean kitchen towel and let sit for 20 minutes.

18. Whisk the egg and milk together and brush it all over the prepared rolls.

19. Bake for 40–45 minutes. I like to start checking the loaves in the oven after 35 minutes just in case.

VALERIA ASHER was born in Ukraine and grew up cooking with her bubbe Tamara. She is a historical tour guide in Paris. When not cooking or giving historical tours, Valeria enjoys forest walks with her dogs, reading history books, and eating delicious Ukrainian food with her husband and their two girls. She shares Paris tour inspiration and information on Instagram @tourswithvaleria and on her website tourswithvaleria.com.

CINNAMON BULKA BUNS

Contributed by Orna Purkin

PREP TIME: 65 minutes, divided | **PROOFING TIME:** 4 hours 45 minutes minimum
COOK TIME: 18 minutes | **TOTAL TIME:** Approx. 6 hours | **YIELD:** 14–16 bulka buns

In South Africa, where I grew up, it was traditional to break the fast on Yom Kippur with a warm *Bulka (a.k.a. Boolke)*, which means "bread" or "roll" in Russian. Passed down by Jewish grandmothers in Eastern Europe, these heavenly Cinnamon Buns are tender and buttery, and not too sweet—perfect for breakfast or anytime with a cup of tea or coffee.

My recipe was adapted from Bobba Skuy's Bulkas in *Es Mein Kind* (Yiddish for "Eat, My Child")—recipes from the Liebenthal and Silber families. I have added modern baking techniques and tips for a foolproof and fun baking experience. I hope making and eating these Cinnamon Bulka Buns brings you and your loved ones joy!

FOR PAREVE VERSION: Use margarine and oat or almond milk

Ingredients:

For brioche dough:
- ½ cup (113 grams) unsalted butter, melted and cooled
- ⅓ cup (63 grams) granulated sugar
- 1 teaspoon salt
- 2 large eggs, room temperature, lightly beaten with a fork
- ¾ cup (183 grams) whole milk, lukewarm (100–110°F / 38–43°C)
- 3 ½ cups (420 grams) bread flour, unbleached, plus more for kneading and shaping
- 2 teaspoons instant yeast
- Vegetable spray or oil or melted butter for bowl

For filling and topping:
- ¼–½ cup (56–113 grams) unsalted butter, melted
- ⅔ cup (126 grams) granulated sugar
- 2 tablespoons ground cinnamon
- Salted butter, room temperature, for serving

Tools:

- Bench scraper (optional)
- Foil (optional)
- Instant read thermometer (optional)
- Kitchen scale
- Kitchen towel
- Large mixing bowl
- Measuring cups and spoons
- Parchment paper
- Pastry brush

- Plastic wrap
- Rolling pin
- Round pastry cutter, 4 ½-inch (11-centimeter)
- Sharp serrated knife
- Sheet pans x 2, 18" x 13" (45cm x 33cm)
- Stand mixer with dough hook (or mixing bowl and rubber spatula)
- Toothpick
- Wire cooling rack

Instructions:

Make the dough:

1. Line two baking sheets with parchment paper.
2. To the bowl of your stand mixer, add butter, sugar, salt, eggs, milk, flour, and yeast. Mix with a spatula or with the paddle attachment on low speed until well combined.
3. Cover with kitchen towel and rest shaggy dough for 12–15 minutes (autolyse). This allows the flour to absorb all the moisture, making the dough easier to knead and require less flour overall.
4. Knead for 8–10 minutes with the dough hook on low speed (or by hand).
5. Scrape the bowl and turn the dough over once or twice. The dough should be tacky, but not sticky, and should pull away from the sides. If it doesn't or is very sticky, dust in a tablespoon of flour. Try not to add too much extra flour or your buns will be heavy.
6. Scrape dough onto a lightly floured counter and knead by hand briefly to make sure you have a soft, supple, elastic dough. Use a bench scraper to help lift and move the dough, sprinkling flour on the counter if necessary.

Proof the dough:

7. Form the dough into a ball. Place it in a large, oiled bowl and press down to flatten (so you can see when it has doubled in size), then flip it so it is oiled on both sides.
8. Cover the bowl tightly with plastic wrap and place in a warmish spot, free from draughts, for 30–45 minutes until the yeast starts to activate and the dough begins to rise.

9. Refrigerate for at least 4 hours and up to 24 hours—the longer the better to develop flavor and bring the dough together. Dough should be completely chilled and doubled in size.

Shape the bulkas:

10. Turn the dough out onto a lightly floured counter and press down to deflate and flatten it with softly floured hands. Sprinkle the top with a little flour and use a rolling pin to roll into a rough rectangle, approximately ¼–⅜-inch (about 1 cm) thick.

11. Dip a 4 ½-inch (11cm) pastry cutter into flour and cut as many circles as you can. Brush off any excess flour. Combine the scraps, cover with plastic, and set aside to rest for 10 minutes.

12. Place about 7–8 rounds on each prepared baking sheet, leaving 1–2 inches between them. Cover the pans loosely with plastic wrap so they don't dry out. Mix the cinnamon and sugar together in a small bowl. Use a pastry brush to brush each round with melted butter (lifting the plastic wrap as you go, then lowering it). Sprinkle each with about one teaspoon of cinnamon sugar.

13. With a sharp, serrated knife, make a slit from the middle to the edge of each round. Fold one piece over and the other piece on top of it to make three layers (see photo). Keep the buns loosely covered while you work.

14. Shape the scraps as above and add to baking sheets.

Top the bulkas:

15. Brush the tops generously with the remaining melted butter and sprinkle generously with more cinnamon sugar.

Proof the bulkas:

16. Cover loosely with plastic wrap and set aside to rise for 30–40 minutes until quite puffy (they won't be doubled in size). Alternatively, refrigerate overnight or for up to 24 hours, then set on the counter for 30 minutes to come to room temperature.

Bake the bulkas:

17. Arrange the oven rack in the middle. Preheat the oven to 325°F convection/fan (160°C) or 350°F (180°C) regular.

18. Place the baking tray in the middle of the oven and bake for 12–18 minutes (depending on size of buns) until golden brown and a toothpick comes out clean.

19. OPTIONAL: A few minutes before they're done, remove from the oven and brush any exposed spots with melted butter and sprinkle with cinnamon sugar.

TIPS: If the bottoms are getting too brown, place on a second baking sheet after about 10 minutes and rotate for even browning. If baking 2 sheets on convection, switch and rotate them halfway through. If the tops are getting too brown, cover loosely with foil. Do not over-bake or they will be dry. An instant read thermometer should register 188–190°F (86-87°C).

Cool and serve:

20. Remove from the pan immediately to a wire rack to cool.

21. Serve warm with salted butter. Reheat at 325°F / 160°C covered loosely with foil, for 3–5 minutes.

Make-ahead and freeze:

22. Freeze in storage bags, removing as much air as possible. Thaw completely and reheat as instructed above.

ORNA PURKIN is a jazz singer, foodie, baker, mom, YouTuber, writer, and entrepreneur whose baking reflects her Jewish South African heritage. She healed her relationship with food by embracing good food instead of fearing it. Orna believes in moderation, lifestyle changes, and finding joy! She shares her recipes on her website ornabakes.com.

CORONA D'ESTER: YEASTED CROWN-SHAPED BRIOCHE WITH DRIED FRUITS

Contributed by Luigi Martell

PREP TIME: 4 hours | **COOK TIME:** 25 minutes
TOTAL TIME: 4 hours 25 minutes | **YIELD:** 1 cake, serves 8–12

This recipe's roots hark back to Catholic Europe via Puerto Rico, where "Three Kings Day" is celebrated with a "Roscón de Reyes." This crown-shaped brioche, decorated with sugar and candied fruit, is a much-awaited holiday treat.

My family's version of the "Three Kings Cake" is a Corona d'Ester. Esther was a Jewish maiden who managed to save her entire Jewish community. She married a non-Jewish king, while holding on to her Jewish identity and thwarting Haman's plan to destroy all the Jews in the Persian Empire. Our family tradition is that the lucky family member who receives the slice of "corona" with the raw almond—skin and all—hidden in it, rules the day!

Ingredients:

For the dough:

- 250 milliliters (1 cup) milk, lukewarm
- 14 grams of fresh yeast (or approx. 7 grams dry yeast)
- 500 grams (3 ½ cups) flour, sifted
- 75 grams (⅓ cup) granulated sugar
- 60 grams (¼ cup) softened butter
- Pinch of salt
- Orange and lemon zest to one's liking
- 1 large egg, beaten

For the marzipan:
- 250 grams almond flour
- 165 grams granulated sugar
- Zest of 1 orange or lemon
- 40 milliliters freshly squeezed orange juice, or 1 large whole egg (according to preference)

For the decoration:
- 1 raw almond, skin on
- 1 large egg, beaten
- Pearl sugar
- Sliced almonds
- Candied fruit of choice (halved candied orange slices, candied cherries, diced succade, etc.)

Tools:

- Baking parchment
- Baking tray
- Kitchen scale
- Measuring cups and spoons
- Mixing bowls
- Pastry brush
- Plastic wrap or clean towel
- Sieve
- Spatula
- Stand mixer (or "elbow grease")
- Whisk
- Zester

Instructions:

1. Whisk the milk and yeast together in a bowl and set aside for a few minutes to activate.
2. Pour sifted flour into a mound on a clean work surface (or into the bowl of a stand mixer).
3. Make a crater in the center and place the sugar, room-temperature butter, milk-yeast mixture, pinch of salt, lemon zest, orange zest, and beaten egg inside.
4. Knead the ingredients together to make a smooth and even dough (it will be sticky at first, keep going and it will come together).
5. Place the dough in a large bowl, cover with plastic wrap or a clean towel, and set aside in a warm place to rise for a couple of hours.
6. Meanwhile, make the marzipan. In a medium bowl, mix the almond flour, sugar, and orange or lemon zest with a spatula. Add freshly squeezed orange juice (you can substitute a whole egg, if preferred). Mix well until a homogeneous dough is obtained. Roll into a long rope, and set aside to put inside the sweet bread later.

7.   Punch down the risen dough and spread it flat on the floured work surface. Form an elongated shape, like a long, flattened rope, and place the marzipan rope in the center.

8.   Take the raw almond and place it somewhere inside the marzipan. Roll the dough on itself, so that the marzipan rope is hidden inside the dough.

9.   Join the two ends of the dough together to form a circle—a crown. Transfer to a lined baking tray, cover with plastic wrap or a kitchen towel and allow to rise for about one hour.

10. Preheat the oven to 200°C (400°F).

11. Use a pastry brush to brush the risen crown with beaten egg and sprinkle with pearl sugar, sliced almonds, and candied fruit, to give a bejeweled effect. For an optional added festive and regal touch to the Purim seudah: bake an additional crown, made from marzipan studded with candied fruit, to place on top of the base crown cake.

12. Bake the Corona D'Ester in the preheated oven for 10 minutes, then lower the temperature to 180°C (375°F) and bake for another 15 minutes, or until golden.

13. Allow to cool and then slice to serve. Remember to look for the whole almond!

LUIGI MARTELL is Puerto Rican-born amateur chef, father of two, and a vital member of the Nova Escola Catalana, a Jewish cultural organization in Barcelona. He has a diverse background in communication, advertising, and public relations, and works as a voice-over artist, radio speaker at *AFN Europe*, and a foreign language coach. Passionate about preserving the Catalan prayer rite, Luigi strives to promote this unique historical tradition within the Jewish liturgical world.

CREAM CHEESECAKE

Contributed by Gloria Kobrin

PREP TIME: 40 minutes | **COOK TIME:** 90 minutes
TOTAL TIME: 8 ½ hours, including cooling & refrigeration time | **YIELD:** 10–12 servings

I grew up with Lindy's NY Cheesecake as my ideal. Sour cream or ricotta cheese doesn't do it for me: my cheesecake is mainly cream cheese and heavy cream. You know it must be great when your son eats it right after you take it out of the freezer. In my home, we refer to Shavuot as the Cheesecake holiday! This cake is rich and creamy but light as a feather. Top it with berries and other fruit or leave it plain—it is always delicious!

Ingredients:

- 1 ½ tablespoons sweet butter, softened
- 1 cup graham cracker crumbs (9–10 crackers, pulverized)
- 2 ounces cream cheese, softened
- ¾ cup white sugar
- 2 tablespoons flour
- ½ teaspoon salt
- 2 teaspoons pure vanilla extract
- 4 large eggs, separated
- 2 cups heavy cream
- 1 pinch cream of tartar
- 2 pints strawberries/blueberries (optional)
- ⅔ cup seedless strawberry jam (optional)

Tools:

- Baking dish with tall sides (large enough to hold springform pan and 1 inch of hot water)
- Foil
- Handheld electric beater
- Kitchen scale
- Large mixing bowl
- Measuring cups and spoons
- Metal spatula with long handle
- Rubber spatula
- Small saucepan
- Springform pan, 8-inch
- Stand mixer
- Waxed paper

GLORIA KOBRIN has been cooking and baking since she was a teen in NYC. She started out writing a cooking column for *The Jewish Week* and running a home baking business. As a mother, wife, and grandmother, she cooks and bakes on a regular basis for family and friends. Gloria created and maintains her website kosherbygloria.com and @KosherbyGloria pages on Facebook and Instagram.

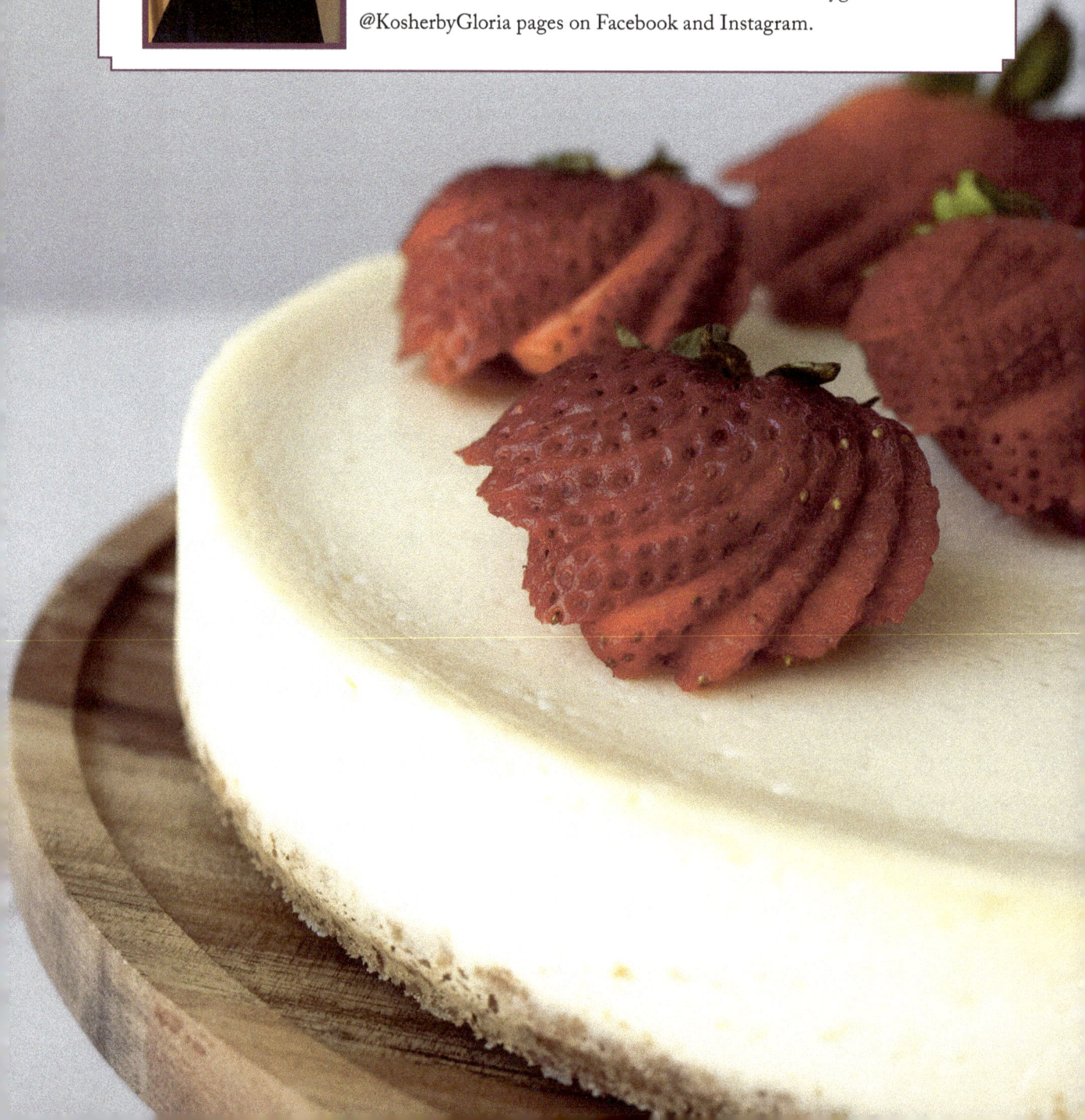

Instructions:

1. Spread butter thickly around the bottom and sides of the springform pan. Sprinkle sides with graham cracker crumbs and pat the remaining crumbs on the bottom of the pan. Place in the freezer for 20–30 minutes.

2. Add cream cheese, sugar, flour, salt, vanilla, and egg yolks to the bowl of a stand mixer. Beat on medium speed until the mixture is smooth.

3. Pour cream into the small saucepan and heat over low flame until the cream is very hot to the touch. (You can also scald the cream for 90 seconds in a microwave.) Slowly, pour the scalded cream over the cream cheese mixture while the electric beater is on low. The batter will be very thin.

4. Preheat the oven to 300°F.

5. Beat egg whites in the large mixing bowl using the handheld beater until foamy. Add cream of tartar and beat until whites are stiff and hold their peaks. Take about ¼ of the whites and add it to the cream cheese batter, mixing together thoroughly, then carefully fold in the rest with a rubber spatula.

6. Take the springform pan out of the freezer and fill it with cheesecake batter. Place springform pan in the ccenter of the baking dish. Pour 1–2 inches of boiling hot water into the baking dish, so that the hot water surrounds the springform pan. Place in the oven on the bottom shelf and bake for 90 minutes. The top will be brown and there will be a slight jiggle to the cake.

7. Carefully, remove the cake from the oven and the pan of hot water. Cool the cheesecake for 30 minutes before refrigerating for 6 hours.

8. Remove the cake from the fridge. Take a long spatula and press it along the outside of the cake around the pan to loosen the cake; then unlock the pan and push up the bottom to remove the cake from the ring. If you lose a lot of the side crumbs, you can grind up a few more graham crackers and press them around the sides. Freeze the cake unwrapped. It is much easier to remove the bottom of the cake pan when the cake is frozen. Then wrap the cake in waxed paper and foil. Unwrap the cake before defrosting it.

9. Serve the cake as is, or arrange whole or sliced berries and fruit on top of it. Melting seedless jam and glazing the berries will keep them in place. Enjoy!

GINGERBREAD CAKE

Contributed by Radka Lím Labendz

PREP TIME: 10 minutes | **COOK TIME:** 20 minutes
TOTAL TIME: 30 minutes | **YIELD:** 8–12 pieces

Gingerbread refers to a broad category of baked goods flavored by a characteristic mix of spices that usually includes dried ginger, cloves, nutmeg, and cinnamon. This moist cakey version is a Czech favorite for an afternoon snack. It's super easy to make so it can be one of the first recipes you prepare together with your kids. To make it extra moist, slice the cake horizontally, put a layer of jam in the middle and let sit overnight. You can keep it plain and top it with powdered sugar, or make it more festive with chocolate icing decorated with chopped nuts, shredded coconut, sprinkles, Smarties, or M&Ms. For a pareve version, replace the milk with plain oat milk or soy milk.

Ingredients:

For the dough:

- 2 cups plain white flour
- 1 cup sugar
- 1 teaspoon vanilla extract
- 2 tablespoons cocoa
- 10 grams baking powder
- 2 teaspoons gingerbread spice mix
- 1 cup milk
- ½ cup oil
- 1 egg
- Chopped nuts (optional)

Optional toppings:

- Powdered sugar
- Chocolate icing
- Chopped nuts
- Shredded coconut
- Smarties
- Sprinkles

Tools:

- Baking pan
- Kitchen scale
- Measuring cups and spoons
- Mixing bowl

- Mixing spoon
- Parchment paper
- Toothpick

Instructions:

---

1. First, line the baking pan with baking paper and preheat the oven to 170°C / 340°F.
2. Add the flour, sugar, vanilla extract, cocoa powder, baking powder, and gingerbread spice powder to the bowl and mix.
3. Add milk, oil, and eggs, and mix again. You can add chopped nuts to the batter if you'd like.
4. Pour the batter onto the prepared baking pan and place in the preheated oven.
5. Bake for about 20 minutes at 170°C, until an inserted toothpick comes out dry.
6. After cooling, decorate your gingerbread cake with the topping(s) of your choice.

RADKA LÍM LABENDZ is a communications specialist and editor-in-chief of *Maskil*, a magazine of the local Reform community in Prague, Czech Republic.

GRANNY RUTH'S APRICOT CHARLOTTE

Contributed by Karen Schneid

PREP TIME: 20 minutes | **COOK TIME:** 0 minutes
TOTAL TIME: 20 minutes | **YIELD:** 10–12 servings

My passion for food was influenced by my Bobba Ray and my Granny Ruth, as I watched them cook in completely different ways and absorbed both my English and Lithuanian heritage. Growing up, my favorite dessert was my Granny Ruth's show-stopping apricot pudding (she even published it in a school cookbook). I've never shared it before, the secret lies in its simplicity.

Ingredients:

- 4 tins canned apricot halves
  (410 grams each)
- 40–45 Boudoir or Ladyfinger biscuits
- Splash of rum (optional)
- 2 tins condensed milk (approximately
  385 grams each)
- Juice of 1 lemon
- 500 milliliters cream, whipped

Tools:

- Bowl or jug
- Chopping board
- Cling wrap
- Colander or sieve
- Glass serving bowl
- Hand blender
- Kitchen scale
- Knife
- Mixing bowls
- Spatula
- Whisk

Instructions:

1. Strain and reserve the juice from the apricots in a bowl, and set aside a few apricots to sliver and serve as garnish. Purée the remaining fruit with a hand blender in a bowl or jug.
2. Soak the boudoir (or ladyfinger) biscuits in the reserved juice. A splash of rum can be added if desired.
3. Add condensed milk to the pureed apricots and incorporate the lemon juice, using a spatula to mix.
4. Whip the cream in a bowl with a whisk and fold into the apricot mixture.
5. In a glass serving bowl, start with a layer of the apricot mixture, then layer the biscuits on top. Keep going until there are five layers of apricot mixture and four layers of biscuits.
6. Garnish with reserved slivers of apricot for decoration.
7. Cover with cling wrap and refrigerate for 8 hours or overnight.

KAREN SCHNEID was born in Johannesburg, South Africa. She practiced as an advocate for 17 years but always had an obsession with food and France. She followed her passion and Ooh La La Artisan Confectionery was born. Today, it is an award-winning French confectionery company. Her Granny Ruth's Apricot Charlotte remains her favorite dessert of all time.

HALVA BUTTER MOCHI WITH PISTACHIO AND RASPBERRY

Contributed by Alana Chandler

PREP TIME: 1 hour | **COOK TIME:** 1 hour 30 minutes
TOTAL TIME: 2 hours 30 minutes | **YIELD:** 16–32 pieces

I created this recipe when daydreaming about new iterations I could make with butter mochi. Butter mochi is a rich, chewy dessert that hails from Hawaii and is said to have been born out of influences from Japanese and Filipino immigrants to the island. This mochi is lightly infused with flavors from the type of halva you find in American delis and Jewish food aisles: sesame, honey, pistachio, and raspberry. As a Japanese American Jewish person, I love making fusion recipes, borrowing ingredients from both sides of my heritage.

Ingredients:

For the jam:
- 500 grams raspberries
- 100 grams sugar

For the mochi:
- 4 eggs
- 500 grams almond milk
- 1 tablespoon vanilla extract
- 110 grams tahini
- 270 grams water
- 475 grams white granulated sugar
- 2 teaspoons baking powder

- ½ teaspoon fine salt
- 450 grams glutinous rice flour (not just rice flour, must be glutinous)
- 115 grams unsalted butter, melted
- 50 grams finely crushed salted pistachios, plus extra for topping. (Place them in a bag and crush them with a rolling pin or pulse them lightly in a food processor.)
- 2 tablespoons matcha green tea powder
- 150 grams raspberry jam
- 45 grams honey, plus extra for serving

Tools:

- Baking pan, 9" x 9"
- Kitchen scale
- Knife
- Measuring cups and spoons

- Mixing bowls
- Saucepan
- Spatula
- Wooden spoon

Instructions:

Make the raspberry jam:

1. Place raspberries in a saucepan over medium-high heat and mash with a wooden spoon. Stir occasionally to prevent raspberries on bottom from burning. Once raspberries turn to a liquid mash and begin to bubble, lower heat to medium low. Add 100g of sugar and continue to cook down until a thick jam forms. Chill and store in the fridge for up to 5 days (if not making the mochi immediately).

Make the butter mochi:

1. Preheat the oven to 350°F.

2. In a large bowl, mix eggs, almond milk, vanilla, tahini, and water with a spatula. Once combined, stir in sugar.

3. In a separate large bowl, combine baking powder, salt, and glutinous rice flour. Mix with a wooden spoon until uniform.

4. Pour half of the wet ingredients into the dry mixture, and stir with spatula until a smooth, thick batter forms with no clumps. (This will be a good arm workout!) Gradually add in the remainder of the wet ingredients to form a thin, silky batter.

5. Pour in melted butter and stir with spatula into batter.

6. In a medium bowl, mix crushed pistachios and matcha. Gradually add in ⅓ of the batter.

7. In another separate medium bowl, place the raspberry jam and gradually incorporate ⅓ of the original batter with spatula.

8. To the ⅓ of the original batter remaining in the larger bowl, stir in the honey.

9. To swirl batters, pour pistachio batter on one side and raspberry batter on the other side of the large bowl on top of the original batter. Slice through the middle of the batter with a spatula and run it around the bowl's edges: do this motion 2–3 times maximum. Do NOT overmix, or else the batters will mix into an odd color! Pour the batter into a lined square 9" x 9" pan and top with crushed pistachios.

10. Bake for 1 hour or until a knife comes out clean when inserted into the center.

11. Wait until it is cooled to room temperature before slicing, and top with honey to serve.

12. Store in an airtight container in the fridge for up to 1 week and reheat in the oven before eating.

ALANA CHANDLER is an avid baker, sharing their creations on Instagram @chow.by.chandler. Alana is passionate about representation of Jews of Color and is currently working on a non-profit community project called *Tlaim: The Patchwork Cookbook*, collecting recipes from Jews with diverse backgrounds.

HAMANTASCHEN WITH MATCHA RED BEAN FILLING

Contributed by Jamie Wei

PREP TIME: 30 minutes including chilling time | **COOK TIME:** 12–15 minutes
TOTAL TIME: 42–45 minutes | **YIELD:** 10–12 hamantaschen

Red bean is a common ingredient in East Asian desserts. Growing up, matcha and red bean was a common pairing in desserts in our house, served with tea. This hamantaschen recipe creates a cookie that has a perfect complimentary taste profile: earthiness from the matcha and sweetness from red bean.

Ingredients:

- 65 grams granulated sugar
- Zest of ½ lemon
- 38 grams butter, room temperature
- 2 eggs, one for recipe and one for wash
- 140 grams all-purpose flour
- 2 grams matcha powder
- 2 grams baking powder
- 1 gram salt
- 150 grams red bean paste
- Turbinado sugar, for topping

Tools:

- Baking sheet
- Cooling rack
- Kitchen scale
- Measuring cups and spoons
- Mixing bowls
- Parchment paper
- Pastry brush
- Plastic wrap
- Rolling pin
- Round cookie cutter, 3 ¼-inch
- Spatula
- Whisk or hand mixer or stand mixer
- Zester

Instructions:

1. Preheat the oven to 350°F.

2. Add the sugar and lemon zest to a mixing bowl and combine with whisk, hand mixer, or stand mixer. Combine the butter with the lemon sugar and mix until fluffy. Add in the egg and mix to combine.

3. In a separate bowl, combine the dry ingredients together with a spatula. Add the mixture into the egg mixture. Mix to combine.

4. Wrap the dough with plastic wrap and place in the fridge for at least 15 minutes.

5. Line a baking sheet with parchment paper. Place the chilled dough on a floured workspace. Roll out the dough to ⅛–¼-inch thick.

6. Use a 3 ¼-inch cookie cutter to cut the dough into 10 rounds. Place the rounds on the baking sheet.

7. Place red bean paste in the center of each disc, about 15g each. Pinch the rounds together to form a triangle (or fold the edges together to get a triangle). Brush with egg wash, sprinkle a little turbinado sugar on top. Chill in the fridge for about 2–3 minutes.

8. Bake for 12–15 minutes. Cool on rack.

JAMIE WEI is a Taiwanese Jewish recipe developer and the creator of chopsticksmeetfork.com. She creates recipes that represent both her Taiwanese roots and her husband's Jewish background.

ABBY FORSTOT SHASHOUA is an Atlanta native and owner of The Fine Print Bakery, which specializes in gluten-free and vegan baked goods. Find the bakery via Facebook and Instagram @thefineprintbakery.

HAMANTASCHEN WITH POPPY SEED FILLING

Contributed by Abby Forstot Shashoua

PREP TIME: 3 to 3 ½ hours | **COOK TIME:** 25 minutes
TOTAL TIME: 3 ½ to 4 hours | **YIELD:** 20–24 hamantaschen

Hamantaschen have always been a delicious way to celebrate Purim. This recipe, which uses a cookie-like dough, is from the synagogue cookbook *The Stuffed Bagel*, published in Columbia, South Carolina, in 1976. My aunt, Sheila Gendil, helped compile the recipe book, and it has since been a staple in our family for decades. *The Stuffed Bagel* includes many beloved family recipes, such as this one.

You can use the basic recipe for Hamantaschen dough with any filling. Some of my favorites are: chopped apricots with jam, prunes, marzipan, honeyed nuts, and berries with jam.

Ingredients:

For the Mohn filling:
- ¾ cup poppy seed
- ⅛ cup butter (use non-dairy butter for pareve version)
- ½ cup milk (use non-dairy milk for pareve version)
- 6 tablespoons sugar
- 2 tablespoons honey
- Pinch of salt
- 1 egg, beaten

For the dough:
- 2 eggs
- ⅔ cup sugar
- ¼ cup vegetable oil
- Orange zest

- 1 teaspoon vanilla
- 1 teaspoon baking powder
- ¼ teaspoon salt
- 2 ½ cups flour
- 1–5 teaspoons water
- Egg wash (for folding)

Filling options:
- Chopped apricots with jam
- Prunes
- Marzipan
- Honeyed nuts
- Berries with jam

Tools:

- Baking sheets, lined
- Cling wrap
- Measuring cups and spoons
- Pastry brush
- Prep bowls

- Rolling pin
- Round cookie cutter, 2–3 inches
- Saucepan
- Spatula
- Whisk or spoon

Instructions:

Make the Mohn filling:

1. Melt together all ingredients (except the egg) in a saucepan over medium heat.

2. Remove a ½ cup of the mixture and place in a prep bowl.

3. In the prep bowl, slowly fold in the beaten egg and mix thoroughly. Then pour back into the saucepan.

4. Reduce the heat to low as you continue whisking until the mixture thickens and coats the back of a spoon.

Make the dough:

1. Mix together all dough ingredients except the water in a large mixing bowl with a spatula, then add the water at the end.

2. Tightly wrap the dough in cling wrap and let the dough rest in the fridge for a few hours.

Assemble the Hamantaschen:

1. Roll out the dough on a floured surface to ¼-inch thick and cut into 2–3-inch circles using a cookie cutter.

2. Fill each circle with a teaspoon of your choice of filling. Use a pastry brush and the egg wash to seal the corners when folding. Place on a lined baking sheet.

3. Bake at 350°F for 20–25 minutes.

HIGH HOLIDAYS BARCHES:
STUFFED SWEET CHALLAH BREAD

Contributed by Marcin Dawid Liera-Elkin

PREP TIME: 15 minutes preparation & 24 hours resting time
COOK TIME: 30–35 minutes | **TOTAL TIME:** Approx. 45 minutes, plus 24 hours resting
YIELD: 3 loaves (1.5 kilograms)

The city of Poznan, where I was born, belonged until 1918 to Prussia. It had a vivid Polish, German, and Jewish community, with its most prominent child becoming the Maharal of Prague. Ashkenazi Jews in former Prussia used to braid their round and sweet challah bread for High Holidays, between Rosh Hashanah and Sukkot. They called these beautiful loaves Barches, from the Hebrew "brachot," which translates as "blessing."

My grandfather Czeslaw loved his New Year's soup made from fish heads, butter, caramelized sugar, and raisins—honestly, not my first choice! But I loved his sweet challah with halva filling. Even during the socialism era, he always had a piece of halva for his grandchildren. It is a sweet treat brought to Poland by Turkish-Polish trade and spread by Jewish confectioners.

Ingredients:

For the dough:
- 20.55 grams fresh yeast (1.5% of the total dough)
- 320 milliliters milk, room temperature
- 80 grams unrefined cane sugar
- 800 grams wheat flour type 550
- 60 grams unsalted butter, room temperature
- 10 grams kosher salt
- 100 grams whole eggs

For the Barches filling:
- 100 grams high quality halva (or poppy seeds, fig jam, or any other filling that reminds you of your family's minhagim and flavors)
- 10 milliliters milk

MARCIN DAWID LIERA-ELKIN was born in Poznan, Poland, in 1980 and raised in Berlin, Germany. At the age of 15 he discovered his maternal Jewish roots, an identity most Polish Jews kept hidden during socialism due to antisemitic campaigns. He specializes in tax law and is the co-owner of Babka & Krantz, the first Jewish master bakery in 750 years of Berlin's bakers' guild.

Tools:

- Baking sheet, lined with parchment paper
- Fridge between 6–8°C
- Kitchen scale
- Measuring cups and spoons
- Mixing bowls
- Plastic wrap
- Stand mixer or your hands
- Top heat oven (do not use an oven with circulating air!)

Instructions:

1. Break up the yeast and add it to a stand mixer bowl, or a large mixing bowl, along with 2–3 tablespoons (30–45 milliliters) milk and a pinch of sugar and stir it well. Put it aside for a couple of minutes until you see foam on top and hear the yeast bacteria working.

2. Add the rest of the milk and cane sugar, flour, eggs, and the unsalted butter to the milk-yeast mixture, carefully. Knead the dough with the stand mixer or manually until it achieves a silky texture. Add the salt in between.

3. Wrap the dough in plastic wrap and leave it in a cold and dry place between 6–8 C for 24 hours. If your refrigerator is too cold, then place it in a cool area of your kitchen where it won't be disturbed for the resting period. The dough will be extra fluffy and easier to digest (FODMAP free).

4. Divide the dough into 6 pieces and flatten them.

5. Mix the halva and milk with your hands or a stand mixer. You may replace halva with fig jam, poppy seeds, or whatever reminds you of High Holidays for you and your beloved ones.

6. Set some halva aside and spread the remaining halva and milk on the dough and roll it into 6 branches.

7. Take two branches and braid them into a round challah (Barches). Repeat twice with the other four pieces to make three Barches.

8. Place on lined baking sheet and bake at 180°C for 30–35 minutes in a top heat oven. Do not use an oven with circulating air, as it can dry your yeast dough.

9. See if the barches are ready by flipping them and knocking on the bottom. A hollow echo is a good sign, and you may take them out.

10. Spread the warm Barches with the rest of your halva milk and let it cool. You may sprinkle your Barches with some chopped solid halva pieces.

ISCHLER COOKIES:
CHOCOLATE GLAZED WALNUT BISCUITS

Contributed by Eva Moreimi

PREP TIME: 25 minutes | **COOK TIME:** 20 minutes
TOTAL TIME: 45 minutes | **YIELD:** Approx. 35 cookie sandwiches

Ischler cookies were one of my childhood favorites I asked my mother to make every birthday. Dating back to the Austro-Hungarian Empire, Ischler cookies were made especially for Emperor Franz Joseph I. They were named after the Austrian town Bad Ischl, where he established his summer residence. A favorite of the emperor, they remain popular in Austria and Hungary today. The tops of these round, preserve-filled cookie sandwiches are covered with chocolate glaze.

During the Holocaust, my mother secretly wrote down hundreds of recipes and shared them with fellow inmates in the concentration camp. Ironically, these delectable recipes were often written on the reverse of papers carrying information about munition manufactured to annihilate the Jews. One of the recipes she wrote at that time was this one for Ischler cookies.

Ingredients:

For the cookies:

- 14 ounces (400 grams) unbleached all-purpose flour
- ¼ teaspoon baking soda
- 4 ounces (130 grams) granulated sugar
- ½ cup finely ground walnuts
- 2 egg yolks
- 8 ounces (226 grams) (2 sticks) sweet unsalted butter, softened (not melted)
- ¼ cup milk

For the filling:

- Jam (I prefer a tart jam, like seedless red currant or raspberry jam)

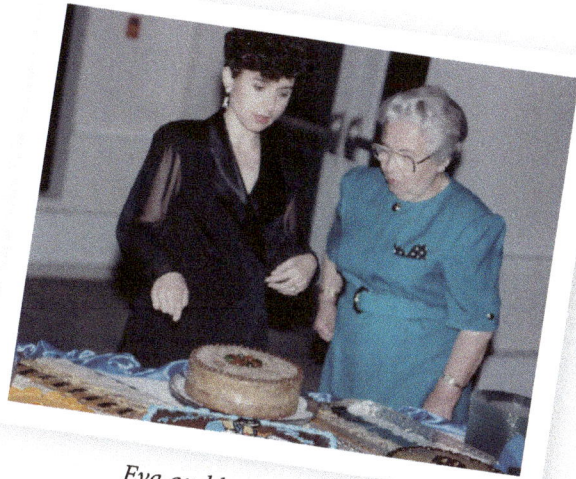

Eva and her mother, 1992

For the chocolate glaze:

- 3 tablespoons unsweetened cocoa powder
- 3 tablespoons sugar
- 3 tablespoons water
- 1 ounce (30 grams) sweet unsalted butter

Tools:

- Cookie sheets x 2
- Kitchen scale
- Knife or spoon to spread jam
- Measuring cups and spoons
- Mixing bowl

- Parchment paper
- Rolling pin
- Round cookie cutter, 2–2 ½ inches
- Small saucepan
- Spatulas

Instructions:

1. Preheat the oven to 350°F. Line two cookie sheets with parchment paper.
2. In a bowl, mix the flour and baking soda with a spatula. Add sugar, walnuts, egg yolks, butter, and milk. Combine and knead with your hands until the dough is smooth.
3. Refrigerate for 10–15 minutes.
4. Roll out the dough on a lightly floured surface, to a thickness of about 3mm or slightly less than ¼ inch.

5. With a round cookie cutter that is 2–2½ inches in diameter, cut out the cookies and place on the lined cookie sheet. Gather the scrap dough, knead, roll out, and repeat.

6. Bake for 15–20 minutes or until light brown.

7. To assemble: When the cookies are cool, spread jam on top of one cookie and then cover it with another. Repeat until all cookies are done.

8. Prepare the chocolate glaze: In a small saucepan, mix the cocoa powder, sugar, and water. Cook on a low to medium heat, stirring until the glaze thickens.

9. Remove from heat and add the butter. Mix well.

10. Spread the warm chocolate glaze on top of each cookie. Allow glaze to set.

11. Ischler Cookies can be stored in an airtight container, with each layer separated by wax paper, and refrigerated.

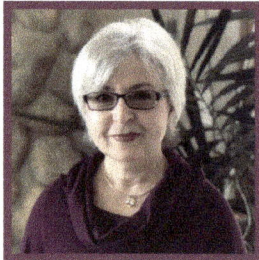

EVA MOREIMI grew up in Czechoslovakia as the only child to Holocaust survivor parents. After graduating from economic school, she escaped the communist regime and immigrated to the United States. Eva's book, *Hidden Recipes: A Holocaust Memoir*, shares the extraordinary story of how her mother secretly wrote down hundreds of recipes and shared them among fellow inmates in the concentration camp.

KANAFE: SHREDDED PHYLLO
WITH RICOTTA AND SUGAR SYRUP

Contributed by Sophia Hassoun

PREP TIME: 30 minutes | **COOK TIME:** 1 hour
TOTAL TIME: 1 hour and 30 minutes plus chilling time | **YIELD:** 1 kanafe, serves 12–15

Kanafe is a traditional Syrian dessert made from very fine noodle-like strands of pastry, layered with cheese and soaked in sweet, sugar-based syrup. My grandmother made it as a special dairy meal every Shavuot in our home in Brooklyn. I learned to make this recipe (and all my other Syrian recipes) from her. Now I live in Israel and Kanafe is available all over the Mahane Yehuda market. In Israel you can even find it in the freezer section of the grocery store.

Over time, I have adapted my recipe, and I use a slightly different filling than what they have in "The Shuk." The dessert is sweet but not overly so and has the signature rose water common in Middle Eastern desserts. I love to eat kanafe with a cup of coffee and some fresh fruit. Delicious!

Ingredients:

For the Shira syrup:
- 3 cups sugar
- 1 teaspoon lemon juice
- 1 cup water
- 1 teaspoon rose water

For the crust and topping:
- 1 package of Kadaif or Kataifi,
  which is shredded phyllo dough in thin strands
  (found in the freezer of most supermarkets)
- 300g unsalted butter, melted

For the filling:
- ½ cup milk
- 3 tablespoons cornstarch
- 1 kilogram ricotta cheese
- 500 milliliters heavy cream
- 3 tablespoons sugar
- 1 teaspoon vanilla extract

Tools:

- Baking dish
- Foil
- Jar or container to store the syrup
- Kitchen scale
- Measuring cups and spoons

- Mixing bowl
- Small saucepans x 2
- Spoon
- Whisk

Instructions:
----

1. First make the syrup. Put the sugar, lemon, and water into a saucepan and let come to a boil, whisking continuously until the sugar is dissolved. Lower the flame and simmer until the syrup coats the back of a spoon, about 20 minutes. Add in the rose water. Set aside to cool and then put in the fridge in a jar or container.

2. For the crust: defrost the Kadaif and pull apart and place in a large mixing bowl. Pour on the melted butter and mix well using your hands or a spatula to coat the strands evenly. Then put about half into your baking dish to form a crust, pressing down.

3. Make your filling by whisking milk with cornstarch in a saucepan and then turning on the flame. Add in your ricotta and other filling ingredients. Mix well over a low flame until everything gets hot and starts to thicken. Whisk continuously so you don't get any burnt spots.

4. Pour over the crust and top with a nice layer from the remaining Kadaif. Bake at 350°F for about an hour. Cover loosely with foil to prevent over-browning.

5. Remove from the oven and let cool for a few minutes. Pour cold Shira syrup over the kanafe.

SOPHIA HASSOUN is a caterer who lives in Jerusalem with her family. She loves her job and living in Israel. Sophia loves to travel as well. She shares her passion for cooking, traveling, and eating on her Instagram page @Syrian_in_Israel.

KUBANEH: SLOWLY COOKED BUTTERY ROLLS

Contributed by Shahar Yosi Elkin

PREP TIME: Approx. 1 hour | **COOK TIME:** 2–3 hours
TOTAL TIME: Approx. 3–4 hours | **YIELD:** 12 portions

Firstly, you should know that preparing Kubaneh is messy but fun work. Kubaneh is a traditional Yemeni pull-apart bread, made from fluffy, buttery yeast dough. It was traditionally baked slowly overnight for Shabbat breakfast.

My maternal grandparents, Tamar and Yehuda, handed this recipe down to me. They were born in Sanaa and Aden in Yemen. My grandfather was a Shochet.

I remember the smell of Kubaneh that my Safta Tamar used to bake overnight for Shabbat morning and how we were 18 cousins fighting over the last piece! After breakfast everyone needed to rest and digest. This is why I strongly recommend, for the full Yemenite experience, not to forget to eat your Kubaneh with a Shabbat egg, Shug, and grated tomatoes. "Shug" typically refers to a spicy condiment or sauce in Yemeni cuisine made with hot peppers, garlic, coriander, and other spices, and it adds a fiery kick to various dishes.

Ingredients:

- 550 milliliters water, room temperature
- 50 grams whole eggs
- 1 kilogram wheat flour type 550 or all-purpose flour
- 29.85 grams fresh yeast (1.5% of the total dough weight)
- 30 grams cane sugar
- 30 grams kosher salt
- 10 grams weinstein or cream of tartar (natural replacement of baking powder)
- 20 grams whole cumin seeds
- 300 grams unsalted butter, room temperature

Tools:

- Container for butter (room temperature)
- Jachnun or Kubaneh pot (any thin aluminum pot with a lid)
- Kitchen scale
- Large mixing bowl
- Measuring cups and spoons
- Stand mixer
- Top heat oven (do not use an oven with circulating air!)
- Tray

Instructions:

1. Place the butter in a container near your work area for easy access.
2. Add all liquid ingredients (including the fresh yeast) into a stand mixer bowl, then add the dry ingredients and mix it on low intensity for about 5 minutes until the dough looks unified and smooth.
3. Transfer the dough into a lightly buttered bowl and leave to rest for 30 minutes at room temperature.
4. Transfer the dough onto your work surface (don't flour the surface) and separate the dough into 130–140g portions. Create a ball from each portion and transfer it to a lightly buttered tray, keeping around 5cm distance between each ball.
5. Let the dough rest for 30 minutes. They should grow around 50% of their size during this time.
6. The next stage is to form each Kubaneh. Lightly butter your working surface, take one ball and stretch it with your hands up to a 20–25cm sheet. Spread a generous layer of softened butter on the sheet, then fold each side of the sheet inwards, add more butter, and roll it up.

7. Take a 26cm size traditional Jachnun/Kubaneh pot and generously butter all sides, including the lid. Put each Kubaneh inside, creating the form of a "sun" while placing each one.

8. Preheat the oven to 150°C (top heat, not convection or fan) and bake the Kubaneh for around 3 hours. When ready, the Kubaneh should have a golden and buttery crust.

SHAHAR YOSI ELKIN was born in Haifa in 1983 to a Yemeni-Lithuanian family. He is a pastry master and co-owner of Berlin's Babka & Krantz, the city's first Jewish master bakery in 750 years. Committed to Tikkun Olam, the bakery operates sustainably with green electricity, energy-efficient machinery, and ecological raw materials. Using traditional methods, they craft heavenly, fluffy yeast doughs with reduced sugar and yeast.

MAAMOUL:
DATE PASTE FILLED BUTTER COOKIES

Contributed by Linda Capeloto Sendowski

PREP TIME: 1 hour | **COOK TIME:** 18–20 minutes
TOTAL TIME: 1 hour 20 minutes | **YIELD:** 24 cookies

I first tasted this intriguing-looking cookie on a walk in Haifa, from Mt. Carmel through Russian, Jewish religious, and Palestinian neighborhoods, past the Baha'i Gardens and Arab stores full of baklava stores, to the German Colony near the bottom of the hill before the harbor.

I stopped for an espresso and a Maamoul, a rich butter cookie with an intricate design on the top filled with orange-scented date paste. A wonderful Middle Eastern, Sephardic, classic cookie, with versions in Lebanon, Morocco, Egypt, Israel, and beyond. You can use a carved wood mold or the tines of a fork to decorate. I make Maamouls and give them away in my Mishloach Manot for Purim.

Ingredients:

For the filling:
- 12 ounces pitted dates (I use Medjool dates)
- 2 tablespoons unsalted butter, room temperature
- ⅓ cup walnuts
- 1 tablespoon orange zest
- 2 teaspoons fresh orange juice

For the dough:
- 2 ½ cups flour

- ½ cup cornmeal
- 1 cup unsalted butter (2 sticks)
- 1 cup powdered sugar
- 1 teaspoon vanilla
- ½–1 teaspoon rose water
- ½–1 teaspoon orange water

For serving:
- Powdered sugar

Tools:

- Baking sheet
- Food processor
- Kitchen scale
- Maamoul molds or fork
- Measuring cups and spoons

- Medium mixing bowls x 2
- Parchment paper
- Spoons
- Stand mixer
- Wire cooling rack

Instructions:

1. Place filling ingredients in the bowl of the food processor. Pulse until it becomes a chunky paste, not perfectly smooth.
2. Remove filling from the food processor and place in a medium bowl, then set aside while you make dough.
3. Measure flour and cornmeal into a medium bowl and set aside.
4. Slice butter into chunks and place into the bowl of stand mixer. Add sugar to butter and start mixer on lowest setting. As sugar is incorporated, slowly increase the speed of the mixer. Thoroughly cream butter and sugar until light and fluffy.

5. Next, add vanilla, rose water, and orange water, then incorporate. (Orange water and rose water are strong tastes, so use them sparingly.)

6. Blend in flour mix and mix on medium low until all combined. Do not over mix.

7. Remove dough from the mixer and form 24 equal balls. The dough should be pliable—not dry—and easy to roll with your fingers—not sticky. If the dough is dry or crumbly add a couple drops of water.

8. Heat oven to 350°F. Form a 2 ½-inch circle of dough with each ball. Place approximately 1 tablespoon of date filling in the center of each circle. Pinch and close the circle around the filling and then roll it back into a ball shape.

9. Place a re-rolled ball in Maamoul mold and press down to fill. Tap the mold on the counter to dump out the cookie. If you are not using a Maamoul mold, use a fork to create a decorative pattern and seal the edges further. Press the fork gently into the dough ball, flattening it slightly and creating indentations along the edges.

10. Set cookies on a parchment lined baking sheet. Repeat until all of the Maamoul are on the cookie sheet.

11. Bake for 18 to 20 minutes or until very pale and just beginning to turn a little gold. Remove baking sheet from oven and remove cookies to a cooling rack.

12. Store Maamoul in an airtight container in the fridge or freezer. Maamoul should be dusted with powdered sugar before serving.

LINDA CAPELOTO SENDOWSKI is a third-generation American Sephardic home cook, taught by her mother and grandmother. Linda's traditional and innovative recipes have been featured in a variety of publications, including the *Washington Post*. Linda has authored a baking cookbook, *Sephardic Baking from Nona and More Favorites*, and also shares her work online at theglobaljewishkitchen.com.

MASOOB BANANA PUDDING

Contributed by Amber-Rose Kedem

PREP TIME: 20 minutes | **COOK TIME:** 0 minutes
TOTAL TIME: 20 minutes | **YIELD:** 3–4 servings

Masoob, also known as malaki, meaning "royal" in Arabic, is a traditional Yemeni dessert. It is made with shredded flatbread and combined with mashed ripened bananas. Eaten throughout the Gulf, it can be served as a breakfast or dessert. Masoob is the perfect way to use up some pantry ingredients that are going stale. For people who are sick of making traditional banana bread with their old bananas, try masoob!

Ingredients:

- 2 large flatbreads (use whatever you like: I often use leftover Lebanese bread, malawa, or chapatis)
- 4 overripe bananas (1 banana per person)
- 500 milliliters double cream
- 2 tablespoons sugar
- 1 teaspoon ground cardamom
- 1 teaspoon ground cinnamon
- 1 teaspoon ground nutmeg
- Pinch of salt
- 1 tablespoon ghee (optional)

Common toppings (optional):
- Honey
- Rose petals
- Mixed nuts
- Grated cheese (sounds insane but it works)
- Nigella seeds
- Roughly chopped dates
- Pomegranate
- More bananas
- Extra cream

Tools:

- Food processor
- Fork or blender
- Measuring cups and spoons

- Mixing bowl
- Saucepan
- Spatula

Instructions:

---

1. Take your flatbread, rip it apart, and blitz it in a food processor until you get breadcrumbs. This is why the bread you choose doesn't matter too much and it is a good idea to use up bread that is going stale.

2. In a mixing bowl, take your ripe bananas and mash them up using a fork. If you prefer a smoother masoob, use a blender to break them down further.

3. Transfer the mashed banana to a saucepan, add and incorporate the double cream, sugar, cardamom, cinnamon, nutmeg, and salt. Turn the heat to medium-high and bring to a boil, stirring occasionally.

4. Add the breadcrumbs into your pot and mix with a spatula until combined. Keep it on the heat for a couple of minutes, or until you achieve the desired consistency. You can also add an optional tablespoon of ghee for a more buttery flavor.

5. Dish up your masoob and add whatever toppings you like. Feel free to get creative! Drizzle with a generous amount of honey.

AMBER-ROSE KEDEM is a Yemenite, Halabi, and Ashkenazi Jewish girl living in Amsterdam. As well as cooking for friends and family, she enjoys backpacking, painting, yoga, and taking care of her many plants.

MAYA'S BOOZY BABKA

Contributed by Priscilla Adams

PREP TIME: 3 hours, including time for a double rise | **COOK TIME:** 35 minutes
TOTAL TIME: 3 hours and 35 minutes | **YIELD:** 2 loaves

A dear friend asked me to put babka onto my bakery menu in Hong Kong, and I flat out said "no." I didn't grow up making babka and felt intimidated. Not taking no for an answer, Maya sent a mutual friend who begged me to bake babka for her husband's 40th birthday. The rest is history.

This recipe is different from many babka recipes as it uses a ganache filling. This boozy babka can be made with any ganache, using your favorite type of chocolate (dark, milk, white, or the trendy "blonde" or "ruby") with heavy cream. Just keep the ratio of two parts chocolate to one part liquid.

Ingredients:

For the ganache:
- 175 grams (1 cup) dark (at least 70% cacao) chocolate, chopped
- 120 milliliters (½ cup) Kosher Irish Cream such as Bailey's Irish Cream original (note that non-dairy alcohol such as bourbon can also be substituted)

For the dough:
- 10 grams (2 teaspoons) dry yeast
- 180 milliliters (¾ cup) warm milk
- 2 large eggs

- 100 grams (½ cup) sugar
- ¼–½ teaspoon salt
- 1 teaspoon vanilla extract
- 500 grams (3 ½ cups) all-purpose flour
- 100 grams (¼ cup + 3 tablespoons) unsalted butter

For the glaze:
- 250 milliliters (1 cup) water
- 400 grams (2 cups) sugar
- 1 teaspoon vanilla extract (optional)

Tools:

- Baking paper
- Cling wrap
- Dough scraper (optional)
- Jar or container for storing sugar syrup
- Kitchen scale (optional)
- Large mixing bowl
- Loaf pans x 2
- Measuring cups and spoons
- Pastry brush (for basting)
- Pastry mat (optional)
- Rolling pin
- Sharp knife
- Small mixing bowls
- Small saucepan
- Spatula
- Spoon
- Stand mixer with paddle attachment and dough hook
- Wire rack for cooling (optional)

Instructions:

Make the ganache filling:

1. Place chopped chocolate into a small bowl.
2. Heat the Irish Cream (or other liquid) in a separate small bowl in the microwave until it just begins to boil. Immediately pour over the chocolate pieces. Allow to stand for 2–3 minutes, then mix with a spoon. The chocolate should all melt. Set aside. Note that the ganache will thicken slightly. It can also be placed in the refrigerator to cool. If it becomes too thick, soften in a hot water bath.

Prepare the dough:

3. Place the yeast into a small bowl. Heat the milk in a microwave at low power (I use 600w for 45 seconds) until it is warm but not scalding. Pour the warm milk over the yeast and mix. Although not required for instant yeast, seeing bubbles come to the top at roughly the 5-minute mark confirms that your dry yeast is active and not too old.
4. In a stand mixer with paddle attachment, beat the eggs with the sugar until thick, creamy, and pale yellow in color. Add the salt and vanilla, then add the yeast mix. Add the flour one cup at a time, beating until smooth and well incorporated. After ⅔ of the flour has been added, melt the butter and change to a dough hook attachment. Add the butter and the remaining flour.

Put the mixer on a higher speed and allow the mixer to run for 5–7 minutes until smooth and elastic. Warning: the dough will feel very sticky but should still gather around the dough hook. Only add extra flour if it appears thin like cake batter.

5. Grease the inside of a mixing bowl and transfer the dough. Cover and allow to rise until doubled in bulk. Pro Tip 1: you can make an airtight seal with cling wrap and cut the rise time by half, to 45–60 minutes. Pro Tip 2: steps 1–4 can be done the night before. Simply cover with cling wrap and place in the refrigerator to rise overnight. Bring to room temperature before continuing with step 5.

Make the glaze:

6. Make a basic sugar syrup by mixing the sugar with the water and optional vanilla in a small saucepan. Stir to help the sugar dissolve. Bring to a boil and allow to boil for 3–5 minutes. Set aside. Syrup can be kept in a jar or other container for 6 weeks (sugar crystals may form at the bottom over time, which is fine).

Assemble the babkas:

7. Line the loaf pans with baking paper.

8. Get ready to roll. Divide the dough into two and weigh to check both pieces are the same weight. Place the pastry mat on a countertop.

9. Roll out the dough: Note that the dough will be soft but should no longer be sticky. If it sticks to the pastry mat or rolling pin, add flour to your hands in small increments, being careful not to over-flour. Shape the first ball of dough into an oblong shape and roll out over the pastry mat. Try to make it the length of the mat and remember, the thinner the dough, the more layers of babka! The width should be slightly longer than the length of the loaf tray. The dough needs to be worked gently to become thin. If too much pressure is applied, it will rip.

10. Fill the babka: Using a spatula, evenly spread a thin layer of the ganache over the dough, leaving ¼ inch / 1 centimeter space around the edge.

11. Roll the babka: Roll the babka lengthwise, starting from one of the two shorter lengths (I usually end up rolling from right to left). If the dough is sticking to the mat, use a dough scraper to help move it along. Don't worry if it tears slightly along the way. The length of the babka will be slightly longer than the length of the baking pan.

12. Shape the babka: Place the babka seam side up. Using a sharp knife, make a single slit in the middle of the roll running the full length of the dough. You will expose the different layers in

the process. Place the two halves next to each other (each length will be just longer than the baking pans). Twist the two sections of dough together, one over the other, the same way you would twist two strands of hair.

13. The second rise: Immediately place the twisted dough into a loaf pan. If the babka is significantly longer than the pan, you can get creative with how you put it in. Ultimately, after rising and baking, the babka will take the shape of the pan. Repeat steps 11 and 12 to make the second loaf. Cover both loosely and allow to rise for 30–40 minutes, until light and fluffy in appearance. At the start of the rise, preheat the oven to 180°C / 350°F.

Bake the babkas:

14. Bake in the oven for 35 minutes. After 20 minutes, baste with the sugar syrup. Baste a second time at the very end when removing from the oven. Allow to cool. The babka can be removed easily by lifting the baking paper out of the loaf pan.

> **TIP:** If the babka sinks while cooling, it means that the center may not be fully cooked (not a bad thing if you like a bit of gooey goodness). While this can't be corrected once out of the oven, try extending the cooking time by 3–5 minutes in the future.

PRISCILLA ADAMS founded The Baking Fairy in Hong Kong to fulfill a community need and spread joy. There's something about how food brings people together that—let's face it—a conversation about financial crime just doesn't. The bakery's motto is "Sprinkling a touch of baking magic over HK." Priscilla started doing marathons to keep baking calories at bay. Running is her happy place.

MEDOVIK: RUSSIAN HONEY CAKE

Contributed by Alyona Lus

PREP TIME: 16 hours | **COOK TIME:** 1 hour
TOTAL TIME: 17 hours | **YIELD:** 1 kilo cake, serves 8–10 people

Medovik has been named the second best cake in the world, and rightly so! Every Russian family has their own Medovik recipe, but essentially they all boil down to the wonderful taste duo of rich honey and smetana, a type of sour cream that is similar to creme fraiche. Unlike traditional Ashkenazi lekach honey cake, this multi-layered honey cake is as light as a feather.

Ingredients:

For the biscuit:
- 165 grams sugar
- 115 grams butter
- 70 grams honey
- 80 grams eggs
- 6 grams baking soda
- 3 grams citric acid (powder)
- 410 grams all-purpose flour

For the syrup:
- 60 grams water
- 30 grams honey

For the cream:
- 350 grams cream (33–35% fat)
- 350 grams sour cream (smetana) (no less than 30% fat)
- 80 grams powdered sugar

Tools:

- Baking paper or silicone mat
- Bain-marie
- Cling film
- Confectionery spatula
- Fork
- Glass mixing bowl (for the bain-marie)
- Kitchen scale
- Measuring cups and spoons
- Mixer
- Mixing bowls
- Pastry brush
- Plastic wrap
- Rectangular or round serving dish
- Rolling pin
- Round cookie cutter, 20cm
- Saucepan
- Sieve
- Silicone spatula
- Whisk

ALYONA LUS was the pastry chef of the famous Moscow patisserie Oui, mon General. Now she lives in Bremen, Germany, where she continues to bake and create wonderful cakes and desserts.

Instructions:

Prepare and bake the dough:

1. Place sugar, butter, honey, and eggs in a glass bowl and set it over a pot of simmering water, creating a bain-marie. Stir constantly with a whisk until the sugar dissolves. Remove the bowl from the bain-marie, add soda and citric acid, and mix until white foam forms. Add flour and mix until a homogeneous dough is formed.

2. Place on cling film, wrap, and refrigerate for 4–6 hours.

3. Preheat the oven to 175–180°C.

4. After stabilization of the dough, divide it into 7 parts of 110–120g each. Roll out each on a silicone mat or baking paper, lightly dust the dough with flour, and pierce with a fork.

5. Bake at 175–180°C for 15–20 minutes or until golden. Remove from the oven and immediately cut the biscuit to a size of 20cm (it is convenient to do this with a pastry ring with a diameter of 20cm). Keep the cuttings and leave the biscuit to cool.

Make the syrup:

1. Make the syrup by whisking water and honey together in a small saucepan. Bring to a boil, then leave to cool.

Make the cream:

1. In a mixing bowl, whisk the cream to soft peaks. In a separate bowl, thoroughly mix sour cream with powdered sugar with a whisk. Add to the whipping cream and beat until a soft cream forms.

Assemble the cake:

1. Put the biscuit on a rectangular or round serving dish (that is large enough to accommodate the cake without it hanging over the edges) and slightly soak it with syrup using a pastry brush.

2. Apply 110 grams of cream and spread evenly over the biscuit. Repeat 6 times and layer the pieces together. Then gently spread the cream on the sides of the cake using a silicone spatula.

3. Keep in the refrigerator for 6–8 hours.

4. Grind the rest of the biscuit into the smallest crumbs using a mixer or rolling pin.

5. Remove the cake from the refrigerator and sprinkle it evenly with biscuit crumbs through a fine sieve.

LETICIA MOREINOS SCHWARTZ is a cookbook author, spokesperson, and food reporter. She is a recognized food personality in the U.S. and appears on network programs such as *The Today Show*. Her work has been featured in the *New York Times* and the *Washington Post*. She shares recipes and virtual cooking classes on her website chefleticia.com.

MOLTEN CHOCOLATE BRIGADEIRO CAKE

Contributed by Leticia Moreinos Schwartz

PREP TIME: 25 minutes | **COOK TIME:** 20 minutes
TOTAL TIME: 45 minutes | **YIELD:** 6 servings

The brigadeiro is a traditional Brazilian fudge-like ball that is made of condensed milk, cocoa powder, butter, and chocolate sprinkles covering the outside layer. As a Jewish Brazilian woman, I grew up with brigadeiro. A few years ago, I created this recipe for Molten Brigadeiro Cake: the cakey exterior has a gooey, indulgent, liquidy chocolate center that mimics the fudgy consistency of brigadeiro.

Ingredients:

For the Brigadeiro Fudge:

- 1 can (14 ounces) sweetened condensed milk
- 1 teaspoon unsweetened cocoa powder
- 2 ounces (60 grams) 70% dark chocolate, chopped

For the Cake:

- ½ cup (1 stick, 115 grams) unsalted butter, plus more for the molds
- 2 whole eggs
- 2 egg yolks
- ⅛ teaspoon salt
- 1 tablespoon (12 grams) sugar
- 1 teaspoon vanilla extract
- ¼ cup (40 grams) all-purpose flour, sifted, plus more for the molds

Tools:

- Dessert plate
- Foil cups x 6, 6 ounces (¾ cup) individual, buttered and floured. (If you cannot find disposable foil cups, you can use six individual souffle molds or porcelain ramekins.)
- Half sheet pan
- Heavy saucepan
- Measuring cups and spoons
- Medium saucepan
- Mixing bowls
- Spatula
- Whisk

Instructions:

1. Preheat the oven to 350°F.

Make the Brigadeiro Fudge:

2. In a heavy saucepan, add the condensed milk, cocoa powder, and chocolate, and bring to a boil over medium heat, whisking constantly.

3. When the mixture begins to bubble and the chocolate melts, reduce the heat to low and continue whisking for another 3–5 minutes until the mixture has thickened like fudge. You should be able to tilt the pan and the whole batter will slide, leaving the sticky fudge on the bottom of the pan.

4. Slide the batter into a large bowl without scraping it. You don't want to incorporate any of the thick residues on the bottom of the pan. Set aside.

Prepare the cake batter:

5. In a medium saucepan, melt the butter over low heat. Pour into brigadeiro fudge and whisk vigorously until smooth. At first the mixture will totally curdle and break. You will think this recipe cannot possibly work but keep whisking constantly until the mixture comes together again emulsified.

6. In a separate bowl, beat together the eggs, yolks, salt, sugar, and vanilla. Add into the brigadeiro fudge and whisk until homogeneous.

7. Add the flour and mix just until blended, using a spatula.

8. Pour the batter into buttered and floured foil cups, filling them almost to the top (leave about ¼ inch). You can prepare the recipe up to this point and refrigerate for 5 days.

9. Bake in the oven for 10 minutes, until the edges are firm, but the center is still soft. Invert onto a dessert plate. Serve with ice cream: pistachio, ginger, coconut, or vanilla are all flavors that work well with this dessert.

> **TIP:** Butter and flour the foil cups well. It's so frustrating when the cake doesn't come out of the cup properly, and part of the cake is still clinging. So don't rely on a thin coating of grease spray. Use soft butter—not melted—and shake off the excess flour.

NO-BAKE YOGURT ALMOND BUTTER OAT CUPS

Contributed by The Jewish Food Hero Kitchen

PREP TIME: 10 minutes | **CHILL TIME:** 30 minutes
TOTAL TIME: 40 minutes | **YIELD:** 8 muffin cups

A healthy dairy dessert for Shavuot that is the perfect portion size. These no-bake yogurt almond butter oat cups taste like a zesty no bake cheesecake. The nutty oat crust is rich and slightly savory and pairs perfectly with the sweet yogurt filling and juicy berries. They are packed with protein and fiber from the almond butter, oats, and Greek yogurt, and they work as a great on-the-go breakfast bite, afternoon snack, or a dairy dessert.

FOR PAREVE VERSION: Use coconut yogurt instead of Greek yogurt.

Ingredients:

- 1 cup small-cut oats
- 1 tablespoon ground flaxseed
- 4 tablespoons almond butter or tahini
- 3 tablespoons honey or agave syrup, divided
- Coconut oil for greasing muffin tins
- 1 cup plain Greek yogurt or coconut yogurt
- ½ tablespoon lime juice (optional)
- 1 teaspoon vanilla extract
- ¼ cup fresh raspberries
- ½ cup fresh blueberries

Tools:

- Large spoon
- Measuring cups and spoons
- Medium mixing bowl
- Muffin tin or silicone muffin cups
- Small mixing bowl

Instructions:

1. In a medium bowl, combine oats, flaxseed, almond butter, and 2 tablespoons of honey. Using a large spoon, mix everything together until a thick dough forms. After a while, it might be easier to mix the dough using your hands.

2. If you are using a muffin tin, grease 8 muffin cups with a little bit of coconut oil. If using silicone liners, you can skip this step.

3. Divide the dough into 8 equal parts and push the dough using your hands against the bottom and the sides of the muffin cups, almost like you are making a tart crust.

4. Repeat the process with all 8 muffin cups and place the oat almond butter base in the fridge for at least 30 minutes.

5. In the meantime, in a small bowl, whisk the Greek (or coconut) yogurt with the lime juice, vanilla, and remaining tablespoon of honey.

6. Remove the oat cups from the fridge and fill them up with the yogurt mixture. Top with berries and enjoy!

From The Jewish Food Hero Kitchen

OLIVE OIL LEMON POPPY SEED LOAF

Contributed by Benjamin Plante

PREP TIME: 30 minutes | **COOK TIME:** 60–70 minutes
TOTAL TIME: 1 hour 40 minutes plus cooling time | **YIELD:** 1 loaf

Growing up in Minnesota, homemade lemon poppy seed loaf was a regular at most gatherings. After moving away as a young adult, I noticed my favorite homemade treat was mostly found pre-packaged at the grocery store or sliced and sold with a fancy latte. Once I moved back to Minnesota to be closer to family, I wanted to bring back this classic kitchen counter treat to share with my family and friends.

Ingredients:

- 1 ⅔ cups (218 grams) all-purpose flour
- 1 tablespoon (9 grams) poppy seeds
- 2 teaspoons (4 grams) ground ginger
- ¾ teaspoon (4 grams) baking powder
- ½ teaspoon (3 grams) Morton's kosher salt
- 1 ¼ cups (260 grams) granulated sugar
- ¾ cup (161 grams) extra virgin olive oil
- 3 whole eggs
- 2 teaspoons (11 grams) lemon extract
- ¾ cup (201 grams) whole or 2% milk
- Confectioner's sugar for dusting (optional)

Tools:

- Baking spray
- Cake tester or toothpick
- Cooling rack
- Large mixing bowl
- Loaf pan, 4 ½" x 8 ½"
- Measuring cups and spoons
- Medium mixing bowl
- Offset spatula or paring knife
- Parchment paper
- Rubber spatula
- Stand mixer (optional)
- Whisk

Instructions:

1. Place oven rack in center position and preheat oven to 350° degrees. Generously spray the bottom and long sides of your 4 ½" x 8 ½" loaf pan. Line with parchment paper leaving an overhang of about ½ inch. Set aside.

2. In a medium size mixing bowl combine flour, poppy seeds, ginger, baking powder, and salt. Whisk together to combine. Set aside.

3. In a stand mixer or large mixing bowl combine granulated sugar, olive oil, eggs, and lemon extract. Mix on low until well combined and eggs are fully incorporated.

4. Add the dry ingredients to the sugar olive oil mixture. Continue to mix on low or combine with rubber spatula until fully incorporated, scraping the bowl to ensure all ingredients are mixed. With the mixer still on low, slowly add milk to the batter. Once added, scrape the sides of the bowl and increase the mixer speed to medium and mix for 2 minutes.

5. Scrape the batter into the prepared pan and bake until the top has risen, golden brown in color, split along the top, and a cake tester or toothpick inserted into the deepest part of the loaf comes out clean, about 60–70 minutes. Let the loaf cool in the pan for 15 minutes.

6. Gently run a small offset spatula or paring knife along short ends of loaf pan. Using the parchment overhang, lift the loaf from the pan and let it cool completely on a wire rack.

7. Once completely cooled, enjoy the loaf as is or dust with confectioner's sugar.

BENJAMIN PLANTE is a baker in northern Minnesota. He went to culinary school on the spur of the moment during a quarter-life crisis. While there, he also followed his heart and converted to Judaism, a path that he started in his early 20s. Jewish family, identity, and food play a major role in creating his Jewish community experience.

PETITE HAWAIJ WALNUT COFFEE CAKES

Contributed by Johanna Rothenberg

PREP TIME: 30 minutes | **COOK TIME:** 35 minutes
TOTAL TIME: 1 hour 5 minutes | **YIELD:** 8 mini loaves or mini muffins

My petite Hawaij Walnut Coffee Cakes are for those moments where you "need something" with your coffee. These not-too-sweet coffee cakes are folded with sour cream, warmed with the richness of walnuts and spices, and covered with crispy streusel topping. I chose to create this recipe with coffee Hawaij, a Middle Eastern spice blend of ginger, cinnamon, cloves, and cardamon that is normally added to coffee. So why not add it to coffee cake? The Hawaij transforms these mini, unassuming cakes into lush, delicate bites you will want to share with your closest friends over afternoon coffee.

Ingredients:

For the cake:

- 75 grams walnuts
- 1 ½ cups (190 grams) all-purpose flour
- 2 ¼ teaspoons Hawaij for coffee spice
- ¾ teaspoon baking powder
- ¾ teaspoon baking soda
- ½ teaspoon kosher salt
- 1 teaspoon ground cardamom
- 1 teaspoon ground cinnamon
- ⅛ teaspoon ground cloves
- 180 grams unsalted butter, softened
- ½ cup raw sugar
- 2 large eggs, at room temperature
- 1 ½ teaspoons vanilla extract
- 210 grams sour cream, at room temperature

For the streusel topping:

- 7 grams walnuts
- ½ cup all-purpose flour
- ¼ cup plus 1 tablespoon dark brown sugar
- ½ teaspoon cinnamon
- ½ teaspoon Hawaij for coffee spice
- ⅛ teaspoon salt
- 4 tablespoons butter, cold

Tools:

- Cutting board
- Kitchen scale
- Knife
- Measuring cups and spoons
- Mini loaf pan or mini muffin pan
- Medium mixing bowls x 2

- Rimmed baking sheet
- Spatula
- Stand mixer with a paddle attachment
- Toothpick
- Wire cooling rack

Instructions:

---

1. Preheat the oven to 350°F.
2. Spread the walnuts (for both the cake and the streusel topping) on a rimmed baking sheet and toast in the oven until slightly fragrant, about 4 minutes. (Tip: place the walnuts for the cake on one side of the baking sheet, and those for the streusel topping on the other.)
3. Remove the walnuts from the oven and allow them to cool. Finely chop and set aside.
4. To make the streusel, combine the flour, brown sugar, cinnamon, Hawaij, and salt in a bowl and mix with a spatula to combine. Cut the butter into ½-inch pieces and toss with the dry ingredients. Moving your thumbs and fingers in a snapping motion, rub the butter with the dry ingredients until pea-sized crumbs form. Add the finely chopped walnuts and toss well to combine. Set the bowl aside.
5. In another medium bowl, combine the all-purpose flour, Hawaij, baking powder, baking soda, kosher salt, cardamom, cinnamon, and cloves. Add the chopped walnuts and stir with a spatula to combine.
6. In a stand mixer fitted with the paddle attachment, cream the butter and raw sugar on medium speed until light and fluffy.
7. Add the eggs and beat them until well incorporated. You may need to pause the mixer to scrape down the bowl with a spatula.
8. Add the vanilla and mix just until combined.
9. Turn the mixer speed to low and slowly add the dry ingredients. Mix until combined.

10. Remove the bowl from the mixer housing and add the sour cream. Slowly fold the sour cream into the batter with a spatula, until it is just incorporated and no white streaks of sour cream remain. The batter will be thick.

11. Carefully scrape the batter into the wells of a greased mini loaf or mini muffin pan. Gently smooth the top of the batter with a spatula.

12. Sprinkle the streusel topping over the cakes.

13. Place the mini loaf pan in the oven for 30–33 minutes, until a toothpick can be inserted and comes out clean.

14. Allow the cakes to cool for 10 minutes in the pan, then carefully turn them out onto a wire rack to continue cooling.

JOHANNA ROTHENBERG is a recipe developer and food writer. She is a New York transplant who now lives in Massachusetts on her modern day homestead with her husband, daughters, dogs, and many many chickens. Explore her latest baking and cooking creations on Instagram @wildheartbakes and on her blog inthewildheartkitchen.com.

PISTACHIO BAKLAVA
WITH ORANGE BLOSSOM SIMPLE SYRUP

Contributed by Samantha Ferraro

PREP TIME: 30 minutes | **COOK TIME:** 30 minutes | **RESTING TIME:** 2 hours
TOTAL TIME: 3 hours | **YIELD:** 34 squares

This Turkish pistachio baklava recipe is soaked in a simple orange blossom syrup that is perfectly sweet and slightly floral. I remember my roots through recipes. This Turkish pistachio baklava taps me back to my Sephardic roots in Turkey, where my mom's family is from. When we traveled to Istanbul, we found different variations of this wonderful sweet all over the city.

Ingredients:

For the simple syrup:
- 2 cups sugar
- 1 cup water
- 1 tablespoon orange blossom water
- 1 tablespoon honey
- 1 cinnamon stick
- 3 lemon peel strips

For the pistachio baklava:
- 2 cups unsalted pistachios
- 1 teaspoon cardamom
- 1 teaspoon ground cinnamon
- 1 teaspoon lemon zest
- 1 roll of phyllo dough thawed overnight (about 20 sheets)
- 12 tablespoons unsalted butter, melted

Tools:

- Baking pan, 9" x 13"
- Damp towel
- Food processor
- Measuring cups and spoons
- Pastry brush
- Prep bowls
- Saucepan, small
- Sharp knife
- Vegetable peeler
- Zester

SAMANTHA FERRARO is the author of *The Weeknight Mediterranean Kitchen* and founder of the food blog littleferrarokitchen.com. Her recipes have been featured in *PBS Food*, the *Huffington Post*, *LA Times*, *Babble*, *Yummly*, and the *Washington Post*. Samantha teaches cooking classes online and in person from her home in the Pacific Northwest.

Instructions:

1. Preheat the oven to 350°F / 180°C.

2. First, make the simple syrup. Add all the ingredients to a small pot and bring to a gentle simmer until all the sugar is dissolved and it thickens slightly, about 5–8 minutes. When done, set aside to cool.

3. Make the pistachio filling. In a food processor, add the pistachios, cardamom, cinnamon, and lemon zest. Pulse until the pistachios are finely ground but not too powdery. Set aside.

4. Layer the phyllo. Unroll the thawed phyllo dough and place a damp towel on top as you work with it. Brush a 9" x 13" baking pan with melted butter on all sides and layer two sheets of phyllo, then brush with butter, and continue until half of the sheets are used.

5. Add the pistachios. Pour the pistachio mixture onto the phyllo and reserve a few tablespoons to garnish the top of the finished baklava. Spread out the pistachios in an even layer.

6. Continue layering two sheets of phyllo and brushing with the melted butter until all of the phyllo dough is used up. Once layered, brush the top with melted butter.

7. Cut the baklava into squares before baking. Use a sharp knife to cut the baklava into 24–26 squares.

8. Bake the pistachio baklava at 350°F for about 22–25 minutes, until the top is golden brown and crisp.

9. Remove from the oven and pour the orange blossom simple syrup all over the top, while the baklava is still hot.

10. Allow the pistachio baklava to rest for at least 2–3 hours before serving so it can soak up all of the syrup. Garnish the squares with the remaining ground pistachios.

RECIPE NOTES:

*   Thaw the phyllo overnight completely. It should not be frozen when ready to use.
*   Keep a damp towel over the phyllo sheets as you work to keep them from drying.
*   It's ok if the phyllo sheets crack or break, no one will notice after baking.
*   There are about 20 sheets of phyllo per roll.

PUMPKIN RUGELACH PIE

Contributed by Marissa Wojcik

PREP TIME: 1 hour 20 minutes | **COOK TIME:** 35–40 minutes
TOTAL TIME: 2 hours | **YIELD:** 9-inch pie (or 64 rugelach)

Pumpkin pie is a quintessential autumn dessert here in the United States. In fact, during the fall months, everything from coffee to Oreo cookies becomes pumpkin or pumpkin spice flavored. So, why not combine a dessert beloved by Americans with a dessert beloved by Jews to create a dessert beloved by all? And thus, my pumpkin rugelach pie was born! The tender rugelach dough bakes with the brown sugar filling to create one of the most unique and yummy desserts you will ever try.

Ingredients:

For the dough:

- 8 ounces cream cheese
- 1 cup (2 sticks) butter, softened
- ½ cup pumpkin puree
- ¼ cup granulated sugar
- 1 teaspoon vanilla extract
- 2 ½ cups all-purpose flour
- 2 teaspoons pumpkin pie spice

For the filling:

- 2 cups cinnamon chips
- 1 ½ cups dark brown sugar
- ¾ cup butter, softened
- 3 tablespoons pumpkin puree
- 1 teaspoon pumpkin pie spice
- 1 teaspoon vanilla extract

Tools:

- Measuring cups and spoons
- Pie tin, 9-inch
- Plastic wrap
- Rolling pin
- Sharp knife
- Spatula
- Stand mixer

Instructions:

1. Make the dough by creaming together the cream cheese, butter, and pumpkin puree with a hand mixer at slow speed until the ingredients come together. Once fully mixed, add in the sugar and vanilla extract and mix to combine at medium-high speed for thorough mixing to achieve a smooth, creamy texture.

2. Stir in the flour and pumpkin pie spice with a spatula until just incorporated (important not to overmix). The dough will be pretty wet but should not be sticky.

3. Divide the dough into four portions and wrap each individually in plastic wrap. Place in the fridge and cool for at least one hour.

4. To make the filling, place all of the ingredients in the bowl of a stand mixer. Mix until it begins to lighten in color.

5. Preheat the oven to 400°F / 200°C.

6. When the dough is chilled, take one of the portions out of the fridge. On a floured surface, roll into a 9-inch circle.

7. Take ¼ of the pumpkin filling and spread evenly over the 9-inch circle.

8. Slice like a pizza to make 16 triangles. To shape, start at the outside edge of each triangle piece and roll towards the center until it forms a rugelach!

9. Complete for all other portions of dough.

10. Grease a pie tin *very well* and place the rugelach in the tin in concentric circles. Once the bottom is full, layer the rugelach on top of the bottom layer.

11. Bake for 35–40 minutes.

12. Let the pie cool for 10 minutes, then serve. This can be made a day or two in advance. Simply reheat by placing the pie uncovered in preheated oven 350°F / 175°C for 10-15 minutes when ready to serve.

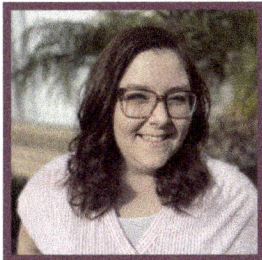

MARISSA WOJCIK is the author of the Jewish baking blog northshoretosouthbay.com where she puts a modern millennial spin on traditional Jewish recipes.

PURAN POLI: SWEET FILLED FLATBREAD

Contributed by Esther Daniels

PREP TIME: 1 hour | **COOK TIME:** 1 hour
TOTAL TIME: 2 hours | **YIELD:** 10 servings

This dessert is made in India for the Jewish festival of Purim. "Puran" means the sweet filling that goes inside a "Poli" (flatbread). The significance of this dessert being served at Purim relates to how Queen Esther kept her Jewish identity hidden, right up until the end of the story. Similarly, the surprise of the sweet filling is revealed only after you bite into the Puran Poli. Our family enjoys this served with spicy potatoes and thickened sweet milk or labneh (thickened yogurt) with pistachios or almonds.

Ingredients:

For the filling:
- 1 cup dry yellow split peas (channa dal)
- 4 cups water
- 2 tablespoons ghee (clarified butter)
- ½ teaspoon fennel powder
- ¼ teaspoon ginger powder
- 1 cup brown sugar (jaggery, if bought from Indian grocer—the jaggery is sold in small blocks, so you need to grate this)
- 1 ½ teaspoons green cardamom powder
- ¼ teaspoon nutmeg powder
- Pinch of salt

For the flatbread:
- ¼ teaspoon saffron mixed and dissolved in 2 tablespoons milk
- 2 ½ cups whole-wheat flour
- ½ cup all-purpose white flour
- ¼ teaspoon salt
- 2 tablespoons vegetable oil or melted ghee
- ½ to ¾ cup of water as needed, to knead the dough

Extras:
- Flour for rolling flatbread
- Butter or ghee for cooking flatbread

Tools:

- Blender
- Cling wrap
- Colander
- Large mixing bowls x 2
- Measuring cups and spoons
- Medium non-stick pot

- Non-stick frying pan or griddle
- Prep bowl
- Pressure cooker or large pot
- Rolling pin
- Rubber spatula
- Spatula for frying

Instructions:

Prepare the filling:

1. Soak the yellow split peas overnight in water.
2. The next day, wash and drain the split peas. Place in a large pot or pressure cooker and cover in fresh water, approximately 3 to 4 cups.
3. Cook on medium-high heat for 35–40 minutes, until the peas are soft. If using a pressure cooker, cook for 10 minutes. The dal is cooked once you can press and mash a couple of them between your thumb and forefinger.

Prepare the flatbread dough:

1. While the dal is cooking, you can start preparing the dough. First, soak the saffron in milk so that a golden mixture is obtained.
2. Mix flour, salt, oil or ghee, saffron-milk, and water (as needed) in a prep bowl with a spatula.
3. Knead with your hands to form a soft, pliable dough. It is ready when you press your thumb into the dough and it makes a lasting impression.
4. Cover dough with cling wrap and set aside to rest.

Continue making the filling:

1. Strain the dal, allow it to cool, and add to a blender. Purée with a blender and set aside in a prep bowl.
2. In a medium size non-stick pot, heat the ghee on medium heat. Add the fennel powder and ginger powder and fry for a few seconds, stirring with a spatula.
3. Add the sugar (jaggery) along with the cardamom, nutmeg, and pea purée and cook on a low flame. Keep stirring the mixture so it does not stick to the pan.

4. You will know the filling is ready when the mixture comes away from the sides of the pan and is soft, dry, and thick.

5. Remove from heat and allow to cool.

Shape the Puran Poli:

1. Divide the dough into 10 equal portions. Form each into a ball and then a pocket, so that it looks like a little bowl. Into the pocket, insert a walnut-sized ball of the mixture and close it up, pushing the dough over the mixture.

2. Maintaining the spherical shape, make sure the filling is fully concealed inside the dough. Now flatten this a bit and sprinkle a little flour on top and onto your board. Gently roll with a rolling pin, achieving a flat circle (8–9-inch diameter), being careful not to tear the dough. Try to equally distribute the filling that is inside the dough.

3. Repeat with the remaining dough and filling, and set all aside for frying.

Fry the Puran Poli:

4. Heat your non-stick frying pan or griddle on a medium-high flame and add a little butter or ghee to coat the surface. Place one Puran Poli on the hot pan for 2 minutes. When you see bubbles forming on the top, gently flip and press down all over with a spatula, frying for another 2–3 minutes. Add butter or ghee as needed. It should be golden and cooked all over.

5. Repeat for each Puran Poli.

ESTHER DANIELS was born in Mumbai to a Conservative Jewish family. The youngest of four sisters, she credits her culinary skills and creativity to her mother, Jerusha. Esther and her Canadian husband, Ken, met at an army program in Israel and have a son, Joshua, together. Esther and Ken relocated from Canada to Melbourne, Australia, where they own and operate the canteens at the King David School.

RHUBARB CRUMBLE BARS

Contributed by Hanna Geller

PREP TIME: 20 min | **COOK TIME:** 45 min
TOTAL TIME: 1 hour 5 minutes | **YIELD:** 8–12 bars

I first made these crumble bars years ago as a way to use up leftover cranberry sauce after a Thanksgiving feast. Now I make them year-round, with in-season rhubarb, fresh berries tossed with sugar and lemon zest, frozen berries or jam in an emergency, or a nice tart apple sauce. There is no need to pre-bake the filling or the base in this recipe—simply binding the rhubarb with an egg and some sugar absorbs all the juices and ensures a crisp base.

These crumble bars are one of my favorite desserts. A cinch to assemble, and they are tart, buttery, and crumbly yet crisp.

Ingredients:

For the crumble base and top:
- 175 grams (¾ cup) unsalted butter
- 180 grams (1 ½ cups) plain flour (or a mixture of plain and wholemeal, wheat, or spelt flours)

- 125 grams (just short of ¾ cup) soft brown sugar
- 150 grams (1 ½ cups) jumbo porridge oats (not instant cook oats)
- 50 grams (½ cup) sliced almonds (optional)
- 1 teaspoon ground cinnamon
- Pinch of salt

For the rhubarb filling:

- 400 grams (3 cups) sliced rhubarb (approximately 5 long stems of rhubarb), sliced 1-centimeter or ¼-inch thick
- 1 large egg at room temp
- 150 grams (¾ cup) caster (granulated) sugar
- 30 grams (2 tablespoons) plain flour
- Zest of 1 unwaxed lemon (or orange when using forced rhubarb in autumn/winter)
- 1 teaspoon vanilla extract
- Pinch of salt

Tools:

- Cutting board
- Kitchen scale
- Knife
- Measuring cups and spoons
- Mixing bowls x 2
- Parchment paper
- Rubber spatula or wooden spoon
- Small saucepan
- Square baking tin, 20-centimeter (8-inch)
- Whisk
- Zester

Instructions:

1. Preheat the oven to 180°C / 350°F.
2. Line the base and sides of a 20-centimeter (8-inch) square tin with parchment paper.

Make the crumble base and top:

1. Melt the butter in a saucepan over medium heat.
2. In a mixing bowl, combine flour, sugar, oats, half of the sliced almonds, cinnamon, and salt. Add butter and mix together with a spatula or wooden spoon, keeping the mixture loose like a crumble topping.

Make the rhubarb filling:

1. Slice the rhubarb stalks into 1cm pieces.
2. In the bottom of your second mixing bowl, whisk the egg and sugar together.
3. Add the flour, lemon zest, vanilla, and salt and mix to fully combine.
4. Add the sliced rhubarb and mix with a spatula or wooden spoon to fully coat all the pieces.

Assemble and bake the bars:

1. Put ⅔ of the crumble mixture into the prepared tin and use your hands to press down into an even layer to make the base of the bars.

2. Spread the rhubarb mixture evenly over the base.

3. Loosely shower the rhubarb with the remaining crumble mixture to make a crumb topping.

4. Sprinkle over the rest of the almonds (if using).

5. Bake for 45 minutes until golden.

6. Allow to cool completely before cutting into bars.

HANNA GELLER is a passionate London-based chef who teaches cooking classes and hosts supper clubs, pop ups, and events focusing on food and design. She is a self-confessed obsessive collector of anything culinary related. Hanna shares her work on her blog buildingfeasts.com and Instagram @buildingfeasts.

ROSE'S CHEESECAKE COOKIES

Contributed by Ronnie Fein

PREP TIME: 25–30 minutes | **COOK TIME:** 37–40 minutes
TOTAL TIME: 1 hour 10 minutes | **YIELD:** 16 cookies

A while ago, I decided to purge unnecessary recipes from the thousands I had collected. But there were a few handwritten ones that I just couldn't throw away. Some from my mom, others from my Aunt Beck, and some from friends and relatives who have passed away. And a recipe for Cheese-cake Cookies from a woman named Rose.

I have no idea who she is or was. My mom had a friend named Rose. Was it hers? I didn't recognize the handwriting on the index card. Unlike most recipes from women of that generation, this had a complete list of ingredients and instructions!

I decided to make them and they are the most fabulous, tender, creamy-crumbly, salty-sweet cookies imaginable. Now, I always make them especially for Shavuot. Thanks Rose, whoever you are!

Ingredients:

- ⅓ cup (75 grams) butter
- 1 cup (120 grams) all-purpose flour
- ½ cup (75 grams) chopped nuts
- ⅓ cup (65 grams) packed brown sugar
- 8 ounces (225 grams) cream cheese
- ¼ cup (50 grams) sugar
- 1 large egg
- 1 tablespoon lemon juice
- 2 tablespoons milk or cream
- 1 teaspoon vanilla extract

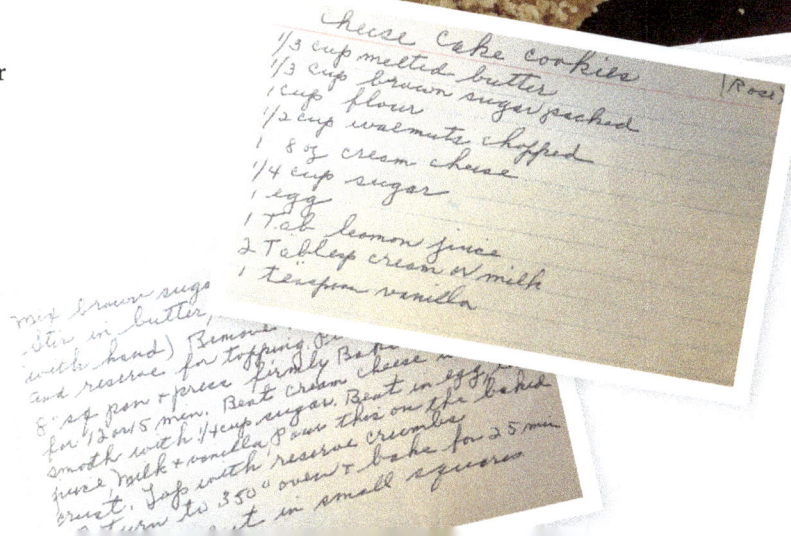

Tools:

- Baking pan, 8-inch square
- Kitchen scale (optional)
- Knife
- Measuring cups and spoons

- Mixing bowls and beaters
- Pan to melt butter (or use microwave)
- Spatula
- Stand mixer or bowl with handheld beater

Instructions:

1. Preheat the oven to 350°F / 175°C.

2. Melt the butter in a pan on the stovetop (or in the microwave) and set it aside.

3. In a medium bowl, combine the flour, nuts, and brown sugar and mix with a beater to distribute the ingredients evenly. Add the melted butter and mix until the mixture is crumbly. Remove one cup of this mixture and set it aside.

4. Place the remaining mixture inside an 8-inch square baking pan, using a spatula. Press the crumbs down firmly to cover the bottom of the pan evenly. Bake for 12–15 minutes or until firm. Remove the pan from the oven and set it aside.

5. Beat the cream cheese and sugar together in the bowl of an electric mixer (or use a mixing bowl and handheld beater) set at medium speed for 1–2 minutes or until well blended. Add the egg, lemon juice, milk, and vanilla and beat the ingredients for another minute or until thoroughly blended. Spoon the cream cheese mixture evenly over the baked crumbs. Top with the remaining, reserved unbaked crumbs.

6. Bake for about 25 minutes or until golden brown. Remove from the oven and let cool.

7. Cut into small squares (16 pieces).

RONNIE FEIN is a veteran food writer whose articles have appeared in, among others, *Newsday, Jerusalem Post, LATimes, The Forward, OU, MyJewishLearning, TheNosher,* and *Kveller*. She writes at ronniefein.com and has authored four cookbooks, including *Hip Kosher* and *The Modern Kosher Kitchen*. Ronnie gives cooking demonstrations and private lessons in Stamford, Connecticut, where she lives with her husband. She has two married daughters and five grandchildren.

RYE BROWNIE COOKIES

Contributed by Avery Robinson

PREP TIME: 15–20 minutes, plus 45 minutes chilling time | **COOK TIME:** 10 minutes
TOTAL TIME: 1 hour 15 minutes | **YIELD:** Approx. 3 dozen cookies

In this recipe, rye adds a touch of earthiness to a classic Midwestern brownie cookie. Rye is an incredibly nutritious and regenerative grain that has sustained communities in northern climates for centuries. Rye, the cold-hardiest grain, is generally known in bread and climate-smart, flavorful whiskey. It is less often used in sweets because its gluten proteins behave differently from that of wheat. This is why rye breads are so dense and why wholegrain rye has such great health benefits! This recipe includes directions to make these brownie cookies Kosher for Passover or pareve.

Ingredients:

- 450 grams (1 pound) semisweet chocolate (55%–70% cacao), chopped
- 56 grams (4 tablespoons) unsalted butter, or 40 grams (3 tablespoons) extra-virgin olive oil
- 4 large eggs
- 300 grams (1 ½ cups) white granulated sugar
- 4 grams (1 teaspoon) vanilla extract
- 3 grams (½ teaspoon) kosher salt
- 70 grams (½ cup) rye flour (on Passover, use matzo meal or almond flour)

Optional:
- 225 grams (½ pound) semisweet chocolate chips
- 65 grams (½ cup) chopped pecans

Tools:

- Baking sheets
- Electric mixer or mixing bowl and whisk
- Heat-proof bowl
- Kitchen scale
- Measuring cups and spoons
- Mixing bowl
- Parchment paper
- Plastic wrap
- Saucepan
- Shallow baking dish
- Silicone spatula
- Spoon or ice cream scoop
- Wire cooling rack

Instructions:

1. Add the chopped chocolate and butter (or olive oil) to a heat-proof bowl set over a saucepan filled with simmering water. Stir until the chocolate is melted and the fat is incorporated.

2. In a separate mixing bowl, whisk together the eggs and sugar until they are thick and pale. This may take 5–7 minutes with an electric mixer or longer by hand. Incorporate the vanilla and salt.

3. Fold the melted chocolate into the egg mixture using a silicone spatula. Once it is nearly fully incorporated, add the rye flour. After the flour is incorporated, you can stir in the optional chocolate chips and/or pecans.

4. Transfer the cookie batter into a shallow baking dish, cover with plastic wrap, and freeze until firm, about 45 minutes. At this point, the batter can stay in the freezer for a few weeks. Thaw before baking.

5. When you are ready to bake, preheat your oven to 350°F. Line your baking sheets with parchment paper (you can re-use it for multiple batches and it bakes better than a silicone mat). Scoop a heaping tablespoon of batter and mound onto the parchment-paper lined baking sheet, leaving 1–2 inches between each mound (these cookies spread). Bake for 10–11 minutes until the tops are cracked and edges look dry. Transfer to a rack to cool completely. The cookie will still feel soft in the middle!

6. Store in an airtight container (like a zip-top bag) for up to 4 days at room temperature.

AVERY ROBINSON is a Jewish culinary historian who works in Jewish philanthropy. He has worked in bakeries in NYC and Tel Aviv, cooked challah for 300 in a campfire, and manages Black Rooster Food, which makes 100% rye sourdough bread. His work with ryerevival.org promotes rye as a climate change mitigation strategy.

SACHER TORTE

Contributed by Nino Shaye Weiss

PREP TIME: 30 minutes prep, overnight refrigeration, 30 minutes assembly
with a 2 hours of refrigeration pause during assembly
COOK TIME: 35–45 minutes
TOTAL TIME: 3 hours 45 minutes, plus overnight refrigeration
YIELD: 8-inch (20cm) cake, 12 servings

The world famous Austrian cake, Sachertorte, was invented by Jewish pastry chef Franz Sacher. He made it for the first time around 1850 in neighboring Pressburg (Bratislava in the Slovak language), where he worked for the nobility at the local casino. The original recipe included almonds and/or almond paste to make it moist. Almonds are still used in classic French Sacher cakes today. However, Viennese versions of this recipe slowly started abandoning almonds from around 1860, in favor of a much lighter cake.

The recipe here requires the cake to be baked the day before serving. This allows for overnight chilling of the rum syrup-brushed sponge, before assembling and decorating the finished cake.

Sachertorte is a spectacular chocolate cake with a shiny glaze, when properly made. It is best served with cognac and coffee.

Ingredients:

To prepare the cake pan:
- Butter, softened for greasing
- All-purpose flour for dusting

For the cake batter:
- 80 grams (2.82 ounces) bittersweet chocolate (85%), chopped
- 85 grams (2.99 ounces) unsalted butter, softened

- 30 grams (1.06 ounces) confectioners' sugar
- ⅛ teaspoon ground cinnamon
- 4 large eggs (approx. 57 grams each), separated
- 1 egg yolk
- 115 grams (4.06 ounces) granulated sugar
- 90 grams (3.17 ounces) cake flour (in Vienna "Glatt – Typ 700")

For the rum syrup:

- ½ cup granulated sugar
- ½ cup water
- 2 tablespoons (30 milliliters) rum
  (I like to use Austrian 60% Stroh Rum)

For the apricot filling:

- 1 ½ cups smooth apricot jam
  (not jelly or preserve)

For the chocolate glaze:

- 160 grams (5.64 ounces) bittersweet
  chocolate (75%), chopped
- 110 grams (3.88 ounces) unsalted butter

For the "Schlag" (whipped cream):

- 4 cups heavy cream, well chilled
- 2 tablespoons confectioners' sugar
- 1 teaspoon vanilla extract

TIP: Double all ingredient quantities to make a 9-inch (22.5-centimeter) cake.

Tools:

- Baking sheet
- Food thermometer
- Glass or heat-proof bowl or double boiler
- Handheld mixer or balloon whisk
- Kitchen scale
- Long serrated knife
- Measuring cups and spoons
- Mixing bowls
- Offset spatula
- Parchment paper
- Pastry brush

- Plastic wrap
- Plate
- Round cake pan, 8-inch (at least
  2.5 inches (6.35 centimeters) high)
- Saucepan
- Sharp knife, small
- Sieve
- Spatula
- Toothpick
- Whisk
- Wire cooling rack

REMINDER: Make the cake the day before you intend to serve it
because the plain cake is refrigerated overnight before assembling.

Instructions:

Make the cake:

1. Preheat the oven to 325°F / 160°C. Brush an 8-inch round cake pan with butter and dust it with flour. (Alternatively, you may line the cake pan with parchment paper.)

2. Gently melt the chocolate in a glass or heat-proof bowl set over a saucepan of simmering water until just melted. Set aside and proceed to the next step.

3. Place the butter in a large bowl and beat with a handheld mixer to soften. Add the confectioners' sugar and cinnamon and beat until creamy, about 3 minutes.

4. Separate the eggs, setting the whites aside in a large, clean bowl. Add one egg yolk at a time to the butter mixture, mixing well with a spatula after each addition.

5. Stir the melted chocolate and check that it is no warmer than 104°F / 40°C before adding to the egg-yolk-butter-sugar mixture, stirring until just combined.

6. With clean beaters, beat the reserved egg whites at medium speed until slightly thickened and foamy, about 2 minutes. Slowly add the granulated sugar, and whisk until the egg whites hold a soft peak.

7. Fold one-third of the beaten egg whites into the egg-yolk-chocolate mixture until combined. Gently fold in the rest of the egg whites until just incorporated.

8. Gradually sieve and fold the flour into the batter.

9. Spread the batter evenly into the prepared cake pan. Smooth out the surface with an offset spatula.

10. Bake in the preheated oven for 35 to 45 minutes, until a toothpick inserted into the center comes out clean.

11. Remove the cake from the oven and carefully flip it out of the pan onto a baking sheet lined with parchment paper, so that the flat bottom of the cake is now on the top. Allow to cool for 20 minutes.

12. Meanwhile, make the rum syrup by placing a small saucepan over medium heat, adding the sugar and water, stirring until dissolved. Stir in the rum and leave to cool.

13. Liberally brush the cooled cake with the cooled rum syrup, reserving the remaining syrup for the next step. Cover the cake with plastic wrap and refrigerate overnight.

Assemble the cake:

1. The next day, carefully cut the cake in half horizontally with a long serrated knife. Generously brush the cut sides with the reserved rum syrup.

2. Place the apricot jam in a small saucepan and bring to a boil, then immediately remove from the heat. Allow to cool, then spread one third of the jam on top of the bottom layer of the cake. Place the other layer on top and spread the remaining jam all over the top and sides of the cake. Refrigerate until set, about two hours.

3. To prepare the chocolate glaze, gently heat the chocolate and butter in a double boiler or in a glass or heat-proof bowl set over a saucepan of simmering water. For best results, heat it to between 122°F / 50°C and 131°F / 55°C. Remove from heat when just melted and stir until smooth.

4. Place the cake on a rack over a baking sheet. Stir the chocolate glaze while it cools to 90°F / 32°C, and then pour all of it over the center of the cake and allow it to spread out. Gently smooth it over the top and sides with a spatula.

5. Place the cake, still sitting on the rack, into the refrigerator for 5 to 10 minutes to set the glaze. Once set, very carefully use a knife to trace around the bottom of the cake to release the cake from the excess glaze, then transfer to a plate.

6. In a well-chilled bowl, whip the cream with an electric hand mixer or balloon whisk, adding the confectioners' sugar and vanilla. Beat until it thickens slightly, stopping before it forms peaks.

7. To cut the cake, dip the knife into hot water between each slice, wiping it dry with a paper towel.

8. Serve with a generous dollop of whipped cream and nothing else. The cake can be refrigerated for up to 3 days.

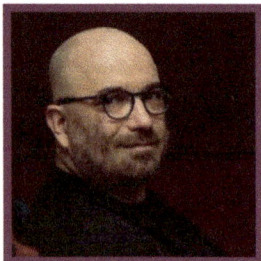

NINO SHAYE WEISS is a food blogger from Vienna, Austria. His blog jewishviennesefood.com pays tribute to celebrated Jewish historical figures like Herzl and Mahler, and the diverse flavors and stories of this once vibrant Jewish Austrian culinary tradition—the lost cuisine of pre-Shoah Jewish Vienna.

SALTED HALVA BLONDIES

Contributed by Victoria Prever

PREP TIME: 15 minutes plus cooling (3 hours or overnight)
COOK TIME: 25–30 minutes | **TOTAL TIME:** 45 minutes plus cooling
YIELD: 16 squares

I love blondies and adore tahina. They make perfect partners. In case you've not met them yet, blondies are the new brownies. Sweet, gooey, and a must-try if you like your bakes fudgy. They're the white chocolate alternative to everyone's favorite dark chocolate bake, and the tahina brings a halva-like note to the party. A touch of sea salt cuts through the sweetness and makes them incredibly more-ish.

I add nutty tahina to everything (sweet or savory), so it was a no-brainer for this bake!

Ingredients:

- 170 grams butter, softened
- 150 grams soft light brown sugar
- 100 grams caster sugar
- 2 eggs
- 1 teaspoon vanilla extract
- 85 milliliters tahini
- 35 milliliters golden syrup
- 210 grams plain flour
- ¼ teaspoon salt
- 150 grams white chocolate chips or finely chopped white chocolate
- 2 tablespoons milk
- 2 tablespoons sesame seeds
- Sea salt flakes, to finish

Tools:

- Baking parchment
- Electric beaters or stand mixer
- Kitchen scale
- Measuring cups and spoons
- Mixing bowls
- Spatula
- Spoon
- Square brownie tin, 20 cm

Instructions:

1. Preheat the oven to 180°C / Fan 160°C / Gas Mark 4.

2. Line the base and sides of a 20cm square baking tin with parchment paper, allowing some paper to overhang the sides of the tin. This will make it easier to lift out the cake later.

3. Put butter and both sugars in a large mixing bowl and beat together with electric beaters until light and fluffy.

4. Beat in the eggs and vanilla and keep mixing until it is pale in color and very light.

5. Add the tahini and golden syrup and beat until combined.

6. In a separate bowl, stir together the flour and salt with a mixing spoon, then fold into the batter with the white chocolate. If the mixture is very thick, add milk to thin it a little—it should be light and spoonable and not super sticky.

7. Scrape the cake batter into the prepared cake tin using a spatula. Smooth the surface (with a light touch) and sprinkle with the sesame seeds.

8. Bake for 25–30 minutes until cooked through. It should be lightly golden with a definite wobble in the middle. Don't panic—it will set. Sprinkle with a generous pinch of flaky sea salt then leave to cool completely in the tin.

9. Refrigerate for at least 3 hours (or overnight) so you can cut it cleanly.

10. Cut into squares to serve. The blondies will keep for 4–5 days in an airtight tin.

VICTORIA PREVER is the food editor of the the *Jewish Chronicle* newspaper, a freelance journalist, and cookery teacher. She lives in Hertfordshire with her husband and two hungry teenagers. She shares on Instagram as @victoriaprever.

SEASONAL FRUIT GALETTE

Contributed by Maaryasha Werdiger

PREP TIME: 40 minutes | **COOK TIME:** 40 minutes
TOTAL TIME: 1 hour 20 minutes | **YIELD:** 1 large 10-inch galette

A galette is a French rustic tart. The beauty is in its simplicity. Flaky pastry with cooked fruit and sprinkled with sugar is a delightful dessert, pairing beautifully with coffee. This pastry has the addition of sour cream, making it more tender. At our bakery in Melbourne, Australia, we use apples in the winter and plums in the summer, but feel free to use pears, apricots, peaches, or any type of summer berry.

Ingredients:

- 240 grams (2 cups) plain flour
- 1 teaspoon salt
- 200 grams butter, cold, cut into small chunks
- 120 grams (½ cup) sour cream
- Approx. 3–4 large apples (or alternative fruit of choice)
- Lemon juice and zest
- Sugar, raw, for sprinkling
- 1 egg, lightly beaten for egg wash on crust
- Vanilla ice cream for serving

Tools:

- Baking paper
- Baking tray
- Benchtop or cutting board
- Kitchen scale
- Knife
- Measuring cups and spoons
- Mixing bowls
- Plastic wrap
- Rolling pin
- Spoon
- Whisk
- Zester

Instructions:

1. To make the dough, pour the flour and salt into a large bowl and use a whisk to disperse the salt into the flour evenly.
2. Add the small chunks of butter to the flour mixture and using your fingertips, blend the butter into the flour until it becomes the consistency of large coarse breadcrumbs.

3. Make a well in the center of the bowl and add all the sour cream. Using light hands, mix the sour cream into the flour and butter until it just comes together like a shaggy mess. You do not want to overmix, which will result in a cookie rather than a flaky dough. If the dough feels too dry at this point, add some extra sour cream until it comes together. Alternatively, if the dough is too sticky and wet, add some flour until it becomes easier to handle.

4. Pour the shaggy mess onto the benchtop and push it all together into a disc about an inch thick. Cover the disc with plastic wrap and put it in the fridge for a minimum 30 minutes, maximum 2 days.

5. While the dough is resting, prepare your fruit. If using berries, combine in a bowl with the juice and zest of one lemon and 1 teaspoon of raw sugar, mixing with a spoon. If using apples, pears, or a stone fruit, cut into wedges.

6. Take the dough out of the fridge, lightly flour the bench (or cutting board) and slowly roll the pastry into a circle, a few centimeters thick. If the dough breaks, just push it back together. Transfer the rolled-out dough to a baking tray lined with baking paper.

7. Arrange the fruit in the middle of the pastry, leaving an inch around the edges. Gently fold in the dough to enclose the fruit, as the picture shows, and press down hard to seal each fold. Egg wash the sides and sprinkle with raw sugar.

8. Transfer to the freezer for 15–30 minutes. Meanwhile, preheat the oven to 180°C.

9. Remove from the freezer and place straight into the oven to bake for 40 minutes, or until the bottom is crisp. If the top starts browning before the bottom has finished baking, cover with foil and let the bottom keep baking.

10. Serve warm with vanilla ice cream.

MAARYASHA WERDIGER is all about bread. Her kosher microbakery, Zelda's Bakery, first drew the Melbourne Orthodox Jewish community to her flour-dusted garage, then from 2021 to Zelda, her two-day-a-week shopfront in Ripponlea. A physiotherapist by training, the world of sourdough lured Maaryasha with its endless puzzles and opportunities for connection. Connect with her on Instagram @z_e_l_d_a_bakery.

SOUR CHERRY SNACKING CAKE

Contributed by Sonya Sanford

PREP TIME: 10 minutes | **COOK TIME:** 45–50 minutes
TOTAL TIME: 60 minutes | **YIELD:** 9-inch cake, serves 8–10

Growing up in a Soviet Ukrainian immigrant home, sour cherries were a favorite ingredient in homemade baked goods and dumplings. Their precious season is fleeting, and the rest of the year you can almost always find them jarred or frozen at Eastern European, Ukrainian, or Russian markets. This simple snacking cake recipe celebrates the jewel-like fruit and can be prepared with either fresh, frozen, or jarred sour cherries. For a pareve alternative, substitute the butter for plant-based butter, and the dairy for a non-dairy unsweetened yogurt. Sour cherry cake makes for an ideal sweet treat at the end of a meal or alongside a morning cup of coffee or tea.

Ingredients:

- 2 large eggs
- 1 cup sugar
- 4 tablespoons (½ stick) unsalted butter, melted
- 1 cup (225 grams) sour cream or Greek yogurt
- 2 tablespoons lemon juice (about ½ a lemon)
- 2 teaspoons pure vanilla extract
- 1 ½ teaspoons baking powder
- 1 teaspoon kosher salt
- ¼ teaspoon baking soda

- 2 cups (290 grams) all-purpose flour + 1 tablespoon, divided
- 2 cups pitted sour cherries, fresh, frozen, or jarred
- 1 tablespoon turbinado sugar (optional)
- Powdered sugar and whipped cream for serving

SONYA SANFORD is a writer, chef, and podcast host specializing in modern diasporic Jewish food and Ukrainian food. Sonya is a regular contributor to *The Nosher*, and her writing has been featured in *Tablet Magazine*, the *Jerusalem Post*, and in Jewish outlets across the United States. She shares her work on sonyasanford.com and Instagram @sonyamichellesanford.

Tools:

- Kitchen scale
- Large mixing bowl
- Measuring cups and spoons
- Parchment paper
- Skewer or cake tester

- Small bowl for melted butter
- Square or round cake pan, 9-inch
- Whisk
- Wooden spoon or spatula

Instructions:

1. Preheat the oven to 350°F. Grease and line a 9-inch square or round cake pan with parchment.

2. In a large bowl, vigorously whisk together the eggs, sugar, and melted butter. Whisk until the mixture is light and fluffy, and increased in volume, about 2–3 minutes. Add the sour cream, lemon juice, vanilla, baking powder, kosher salt, and baking soda, and whisk together until fully incorporated.

3. Add 2 cups of flour to the bowl, and using a wooden spoon or spatula, mix the batter until just combined and mostly smooth—be careful not to overmix.

4. Dust the pitted cherries in the remaining tablespoon of flour. This helps the cherries from sinking to the bottom of the cake. Add the dusted cherries to the bowl, and mix until just evenly incorporated.

5. Transfer to the lined and greased baking pan. Top with the turbinado sugar and a few extra cherries, if desired.

6. Bake for 45–50 minutes, or until golden brown on top, and a small skewer or cake tester comes out clean.

7. Cool and serve topped with powdered sugar or whipped cream. Keeps for 3–4 days stored covered at room temperature.

SOUR CREAM MARBLE CAKE

Contributed by Naomi Althaus

PREP TIME: 20 minutes | **COOK TIME:** 1 hour
TOTAL TIME: 1 hour 20 minutes | **YIELD:** 1 cake

I first made this sour cream marble cake recipe for the bris of my best friend's firstborn son. It's been 27 years since then and those same people always ask me to make this cake. The special ingredients include sour cream, vanilla essence, and chocolate. This swirled cake is baked in a bundt pan, so it looks special and tastes old fashioned.

Ingredients:

- ¼–⅓ cup sugar (to coat the bundt pan)
- 250 grams butter
- 2 ½ cups sugar
- 6 eggs
- 3 cups plain flour

- ¼ teaspoon salt
- ½ teaspoon bicarbonate soda
- 1 ¼ cups sour cream
- 2 teaspoons vanilla essence
- 8 ounces chocolate

Tools:

- Angel cake tin (bundt pan)
- Fork
- Kitchen scale
- Measuring cups and spoons
- Non-stick spray
- Sieve
- Small mixing bowl
- Spatula
- Stand mixer

Instructions:

1. Spray an angel cake tin with non-stick spray and coat with sugar generously, then set aside.
2. In a mixer, beat the butter and sugar and slowly add the eggs.
3. Sift the flour, salt, and bicarbonate soda and add to the egg mix with sour cream and vanilla essence. Beat until combined.
4. Melt the chocolate.
5. Pour just over half the cake batter into the tin.
6. Mix the melted chocolate with the remaining cake mixture and pour it into the tin.
7. Run your fork through the mixture to swirl the dark and light colors, creating a marble effect.
8. Bake at 350°F for 1 hour. Depending on your oven it may need longer.

NAOMI ALTHAUS loved baking from a young age, often bringing homemade cakes to school celebrations. She collected recipes and skills through travels to Israel, the U.S., and Europe. Together with family recipes, they became the foundation for her boutique catering business in Australia. Twenty-five years later, married with three grown children, Naomi still loves creating delicacies from simple butter, sugar, and flour.

SUFGANIYOT WITH VANILLA CUSTARD FILLING

Contributed by Aviva Tal-Ohr

PREP TIME: 1 hour 20 minutes | **COOK TIME:** 30 minutes
TOTAL TIME: 1 hour 50 minutes | **YIELD:** 20 sufganiyot

Sufganiyot are delicious, pillowy "Jewish" doughnuts. Deep fried and filled with jam or custard, they are eaten in Israel and around the world during Chanukah. This recipe includes a rich, velvety, and delicate vanilla custard. Your family and friends will be super impressed by your gourmet sufganiyot.

Ingredients:

- 4 cups flour
- ½ cup sugar
- Pinch of salt
- 1 teaspoon yeast
- 1 cup warm water
- 1 teaspoon vanilla essence
- 1 egg
- ¼ cup vegetable oil
- Optional decorations: Icing sugar, sprinkles

- Optional fillings: Dulce de Leche, Nutella spread, custard

For the vanilla custard filling:

- 6 egg yolks
- ⅔ cup sugar
- 1 tablespoon vanilla essence
- 2 tablespoons cornflour
- 2 cups milk
- 1 tablespoon butter

Tools:

- Kebab stick or straw
- Large frying pan
- Measuring cups and spoons
- Metal slotted spoon
- Mixing bowls
- Saucepan
- Whisk

Instructions:

1. Combine flour, sugar, salt, yeast, water, vanilla, egg, and oil. You can do this on a clean work-top or in a bowl. Whisk ingredients together.

2. Knead for 10 minutes to form a nice, soft dough that isn't too sticky. Place in an oiled bowl. Cover and leave to rise in a warm place for at least 1 hour.

3. Form dough into 20 equal size balls. Leave to rise for about 20 minutes.

4. In a large frying pan, heat oil to 180°C. Fry the doughnut balls for 2 minutes on each side, until golden. Depending on the size of your frying pan, you might need to fry the doughnut balls in batches.

5. Remove from oil with a metal slotted spoon and allow to cool. Wait until completely cool before adding filling.

6. Use a kebab stick or straw to poke a hole in each doughnut.

7. Fill the doughnut with filling of choice and decorate.

To make the custard filling:

1. Separate egg yolks from egg whites and place in a medium mixing bowl. Set aside the whites to use in another recipe.

2. Add sugar and vanilla essence to the egg yolks and whisk until combined. Add cornflour and mix well.

3. Warm milk over medium heat (don't boil), then add the butter.

4. Remove milk from heat. Allow to slightly cool.

5. Gradually add the warm milk, a bit at a time, to the egg yolk mixture, whisking all the time. Continue until all milk is incorporated.

6. Transfer the mixture back to the saucepan and heat on a low flame while continuously whisking. Stir until the consistency thickens and the mixture turns a darker shade of yellow.

7. Remove from heat. Allow to cool completely in the fridge. Your custard is now ready to use!

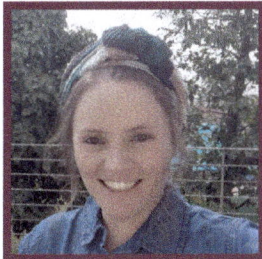

AVIVA TAL-OHR is a full-time working mommy and cooking enthusiast. She lives in Israel with her husband and 3 young children, whom she loves to cook with. She believes that some of the best memories are made in the kitchen. Aviva runs a cooking channel on YouTube @AvivaTalOhr.

SUTLACH RICE PUDDING

Contributed by Susan Barocas

PREP TIME: 5 minutes | **COOK TIME:** 15 minutes
TOTAL TIME: 20 minutes | **YIELD:** 4–6 servings

Turkish Sütlach is served throughout the Mediterranean and Middle East and beloved by Sephardim. The older generation may fondly remember individual servings decorated with children's initials, spelled out in cinnamon by mothers and grandmothers. Sutlach was traditionally prepared in advance and served for Shabbat breakfast and to break the fast after Yom Kippur. Instead of milk, sometimes pipitada (made from soaking ground melon seeds in water for 24 hours) was added. For a pareve alternative, use plant-based milk.

Traditionally, this creamy pudding may be made with either rice grains or the quicker rice flour used here. The vanilla and orange zest can be swapped for a more traditional 1 to 2 teaspoons orange blossom or rose water. A sprinkling of chopped pistachios adds a nice crunch.

Ingredients:

- ½ cup rice flour, white or brown
- ½ cup sugar
- ⅓ cup water (approx.)
- 4 cups milk
- 1 teaspoon vanilla extract
- 1 tablespoon grated orange zest or 1 teaspoon orange blossom or rose water (optional)
- Ground cinnamon
- Finely chopped pistachios (optional)

Tools:

- Custard cups or small bowls
- Measuring cups and spoons
- Medium bowl
- Medium saucepan
- Whisk
- Wooden spoon

Instructions:

1. In a medium bowl, whisk together the rice flour and sugar. Whisking constantly, slowly add just enough water to form a thick, smooth paste.

2. In a saucepan over medium heat, bring the milk just to boiling point—when you can see little bubbles starting to form around the edge. Do not let it boil.

3. To keep lumps from forming, stir with a wooden spoon or whisk constantly as you slowly and steadily add the rice-flour paste to the milk.

4. Keep stirring constantly until it thickens, about 10 minutes. Lower the heat if needed to keep the mixture from boiling.

5. Remove from the heat and stir in the vanilla and orange zest or rose water. Pour into custard cups or small bowls for individual servings.

6. Sprinkle with cinnamon, especially in initials, Hebrew letters, or other designs. As another option, sprinkle with the finely chopped pistachios.

7. Let cool on the counter and serve at room temperature or refrigerate until chilled. Keep refrigerated and serve within 2 days.

SUSAN BAROCAS is a writer, chef, cooking instructor, and speaker. She is passionate about healthy, reduced-waste cooking and Jewish food, especially Sephardic history, cultures, and cuisines. Founding director of the innovative Jewish Food Experience, she served as guest chef for three of President Obama's White House Seders. Susan is co-founder/co-director of Savor: A Sephardic Music & Food Experience.

TEREZIN LEGACY NUT BRAID

Contributed by Toby Colton

PREP TIME: 1–2 hours, plus 5 hours chilling time (or overnight)
COOK TIME: 30 minutes | **TOTAL TIME:** 8+ hours
YIELD: 2 very large braids, about 40 slices

This recipe is an adaptation from *In Memory's Kitchen*, a cookbook from Terezin, also known as Theresienstadt, written by imprisoned women being starved. The recipes, originally in Yiddish, were incomplete, with English translations offering occasional hints. Among them, I discovered a recipe for Nuss Zopf, or "Nut Braid," which seemed relatively complete. Translating it, I felt a profound connection to the baker.

I embarked on making it, deeply moved by the idea that turning this into a functional recipe ensured the woman behind it would not be forgotten. As I worked, I felt her skilled presence guiding me. I hope both women and men will consider baking this loaf. In doing so, we honor the women who may have no one to remember them or say Kaddish for them.

TIPS:

- **You need a cold kitchen!** I strongly suggest that you don't try to make it if your kitchen is warm and if you do not have a refrigerator in which to put the dough between folding. Keeping the butter firm, not melting, is key to the lovely layers that develop and the lightness of the loaf.
- **Handle the dough gently!** While you knead the dough briefly, you are not making a sandwich loaf. You want layers to develop, so always handle the dough gently.
- **Have plenty of time!** Lastly, it can take a whole day to make it from start to finish. It can be refrigerated at a stopping point overnight so that it takes parts of two days.
- **Be sure to measure!** To ensure consistency, I recommend using a ruler and yardstick to measure the length of the butter pat and dough to make sure you're shaping everything to the correct size.

Ingredients:

For the dough:
- 2 packages or 4 ½ teaspoons active dry yeast
- ¼ cup warm water
- 6–7 cups unbleached all-purpose flour, plus more for light dusting
- ½ cup granulated sugar
- 1 cup whole milk
- 2 large eggs
- 2 teaspoons table or sea salt (not kosher salt)

For the butter pat or inlay:
- ⅓ cup unbleached all-purpose flour
- 1 ½ cups (3 sticks) cold unsalted butter

For the filling:
- 2 cups raisins
- 1 ½ cups finely chopped walnuts, pecans, and/or almonds
- 1 ¼ cups granulated sugar
- ¾ cup finely chopped, or snipped with scissors, dried (tart) apricots (about 15-20)
- ½ cup (1 stick) butter, melted

- ¼ cup grated bittersweet chocolate or to taste (*I found it easier to freeze semi-sweet chocolate chips and then put them into a food processor—mini works well—and then process with about ½ cup of the granulated sugar.*)
- 2–2 ½ tablespoons ground cinnamon

For the topping:
- 2 tablespoons melted butter, cooled
- 1 large egg, beaten, at room temperature
- Coarse sugar (optional)

For the icing (optional):
- 2 cups sifted powdered sugar (approx.)
- ¼ cup milk, at room temperature
- 2 tablespoons butter, softened at room temperature, or melted
- ½ teaspoon vanilla extract

NOTE: You can add your own personal touch or ingredients to the filling.

Tools:

- Cookie sheets (mine are 16 ½" x 13 ½")
- Dough scraper (optional)
- Food processor or pastry blender (optional)
- Measuring cups and spoons
- Mixing bowls
- Parchment paper, and/or large pastry rolling mat, or another surface such as a wooden surface on which to roll out the dough
- Pastry brush
- Plastic wrap
- Rolling pin
- Ruler and yardstick
- Scissors
- Sharp knife
- Sharp tooth edge knife
- Small bowls x 6
- Small saucepan
- Stand mixer
- Wax paper (optional)
- Wood cutting board

Instructions:

Make the dough:

1. In a large bowl of an electric mixer, stir the yeast into the warm water. Let rest until some bubbling has occurred, at least 5 minutes.
2. Add 2 cups of the flour, sugar, milk, eggs, and salt and beat with the dough hook of the mixer for 2 minutes. Gradually work in enough additional flour to make a soft, slightly sticky dough.
3. Remove the dough from the bowl to a flat work surface. Knead until smooth and elastic, 5–8 minutes. (I use a dough scraper in one hand for this part of the process to lift the dough from the work surface because it tends to stick.)
4. Wrap dough loosely in plastic wrap and chill at least 15 minutes—longer is better.

While the dough rests, make the butter pat:

5. Using a heavy-duty mixer, food processor, or pastry blender, combine flour with cold butter until smooth. Do not cream it completely or overmix; some lumps are desirable. You do not want to beat air into the mixture.
6. Flatten butter mixture between two sheets of wax paper, plastic wrap, or parchment paper into a 9" x 12" rectangle, using a rolling pin.
7. Chill until firm but not hard, about 30 minutes.

Make the filling:

8. Combine all the filling ingredients and set aside. You will have about 6 cups. (I like to divide this into 6 equal portions so that the last one does not come up short.)

Finish the dough:

9. Roll out the dough: Remove dough from the refrigerator. Roll into a large rectangle, about 7 inches wide and as long as necessary to make it about ½-inch thick (about 20–22 inches).

10. Cut the butter pat crosswise and place one half on the center one-third of the dough.

11. Fold one long end down over the butter.

12. Place the remaining butter pat on top of folded dough.

13. Fold remaining dough flap up over the butter pat (the same procedure used to make croissants).

14. Gently pinch edges to seal in butter.

15. Turn the dough one-quarter turn so that one sealed edge is facing you.

16. With your rolling pin, gently roll dough into a rectangle about 8" x 24". Fold dough in thirds to form a square of about 8" x 8". If the dough or butter is too warm, chill dough for a few minutes so that butter does not leak out. (If butter shows through in some spots, pat a little flour over the butter and continue the procedure.)

17. Wrap in plastic and chill for at least 20 minutes. More time is better—35–40 minutes is about right.

18. Repeat this rolling out and folding procedure twice more for a total of three times. Each time, begin with a folded edge facing you so that you roll it in the opposite way from when it was the previous time. It is important to keep dough chilled, so roll it as soon as you remove it from the refrigerator and then return it to the refrigerator as soon as you are done.

19. At this point, dough can be wrapped and chilled overnight. Otherwise, chill for at least 30–40 minutes. The longer the dough chills, the easier it is to roll it out and fill it.

Assemble the nut braid:

20. Remove dough from the refrigerator and cut it in half using a toothed edge knife with a gentle sawing motion.

21. Wrap and refrigerate one half. Cut the other half of the dough into 3 equal parts. Roll out one part into a 10-inch square, pressing on the floured (top) side, not the cut side.

22. Wet the sides and bottom edge lightly with your fingers. Keeping the filling about 1 inch away from the edges, sprinkle with one-sixth of the filling (about 1 cup).

23. Roll up jelly roll or strudel-style, brushing off any excess flour with a pastry brush as you go.

24. Gently pinch the side seams together as you roll, then pinch the end seam together; use a little water on the dough if necessary to get a good seal. Place seam side down. Repeat with the other two parts.

25. Now turn one of the pieces so that one of the round ends is toward you and the other is facing away from you. Roll out the dough piece into a long thin strip, no longer than 16 inches. Pieces of the filling may show through a little. It will be long and flat.

26. Turn your dough so that the long edge is closest to you. Starting with that edge, roll it up by hand so that it is tubular, instead of flat. Place on a large greased or parchment-lined cookie sheet. It cannot be longer than the diagonal length of your cookie sheet.)

27. Repeat with the other two pieces, keeping them the same length as the first one. Place the other two pieces on the cookie sheet parallel to the first and do a simple braid, tucking both ends under.

28. Dust lightly with flour and cover gently with plastic wrap and let rise 1–3 hours at room temperature, or until puffed (the time depends on the type of yeast and room temperature).

29. Repeat all these steps with the second half of the dough.

30. Preheat the oven to 375°F.

31. Brush braids gently with a topping mixture of melted butter and beaten egg and, if desired, sprinkle with optional coarse sugar.

32. Bake loaves in a preheated oven for 20–30 minutes, or until they are a very deep golden brown and baked through. Tent with foil for the last 15–20 minutes if the braid is browning too quickly. The loaves may split down the braid lines exposing the filling. Let cool completely on cookie sheets.

33. If desired, combine the icing ingredients and spread or drizzle over the cooled nut braids.

34. Serve fresh or freeze to enjoy another time.

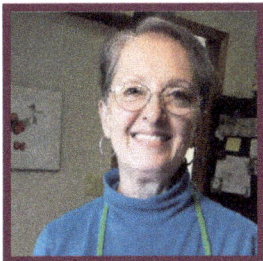

TOBY COLTON, now in her late seventies, fell in love with food and cooking at age six with a children's cookbook. With an extensive collection boasting hundreds of titles, she continues to explore and celebrate the diverse realms of culinary literature.

PAREVE RECIPES

APPLE CHOCOLATE CHIP CAKE

Contributed by Mari Levine

PREP TIME: 10 minutes | **COOK TIME:** 1 hour 10 minutes
TOTAL TIME: 1 hour 20 minutes | **YIELD:** 14 servings

This apple chocolate chip cake has been a staple in my life—and in my mother Gale's recipe box—for as long as I can remember. Its origins have been lost to time, but my mom suspects she got it from a dear friend many decades ago. Since then, it's become her go-to recipe for its ease and versatility. (She usually prepares it in a tube pan, as I do here, but it can also be made in loaf pans.) It's served at just about every family gathering. It's gifted to friends when they're celebrating or mourning. It represents tradition and comfort, and it's a favorite in my family's home. I hope it becomes one in yours too.

Ingredients:

- 3 large eggs
- ¾ cup (150 grams) canola oil
- 1 ½ cups (300 grams) sugar
- 2 cups (280 grams) flour
- 1 teaspoon baking soda
- 5 medium apples (McIntosh, Gala, or your favorite sweet apple), peeled, cored, and chopped coarsely into ¼–½-inch pieces (about 5 cups or 600 grams)
- ¾ cup (120 grams) semisweet or milk chocolate chocolate chips

Tools:

- Baking spray
- Chef's knife
- Cooling rack
- Cutting board
- Large mixing bowl
- Measuring cups and spoons
- Silicone spatula or wooden spoon
- Toothpick
- Tube pan (also known as a bundt pan, or alternatively use two loaf pans)

Instructions:

1. Preheat the oven to 350°F / 175°C. Spray tube pan with baking spray.

2. In a large bowl, mix together the eggs, oil, and sugar until smooth.

3. Stir in the flour and baking soda until combined, then fold in the chopped apples.

4. Stir in the chocolate chips.

5. Transfer to the prepared tube pan.

6. Bake on the middle rack until the top of the cake starts to turn golden brown and a toothpick inserted in the center comes out with only a few crumbs attached, about an hour and 10 minutes.

7. Transfer to a cooling rack and allow to cool to room temperature.

8. To remove from the pan, run a knife between pan and cake, and invert the pan on a plate. Give the bottom of the pan a few smacks with a wooden spoon and the cake should come out smoothly.

9. The cake lasts up to 4 days wrapped in aluminum foil and kept at room temperature.

MARI LEVINE is a writer and editor who has spent her career working with food and writing about it for outlets such as *America's Test Kitchen* and *JewishBoston.com*. When not eating or cooking, she can be found biking, volunteering in her community, or learning a new sport. She lives in Boston, Massachusetts, with her partner and their cat.

AUNT ESTER'S MANDARIN POPPY SEED PUDDING CAKE

Contributed by Vero Najmias

PREP TIME: 20 minutes | **COOK TIME:** 45 minutes
TOTAL TIME: 65 minutes | **YIELD:** 12 servings

Like many, my single apartment started with just a mattress and a pan. Looking for a quick, simple, and inexpensive recipe, I asked my loving Tia Ester for her favorite recipe: Mandarin and Poppy Seed Pudding Cake. With only one bowl, we can solve almost everything. She adored the mandarin version—me too—but you can replace it with lemons, oranges, bergamot, or a mix. If you don't have poppy seeds, feel free to skip them. Ideal for a Sunday afternoon!

Ingredients:

- 2 cups (380 grams) sugar
- 1 cup (210 milliliters) neutral oil
- 2 eggs at room temperature
- 2 mandarins, well washed with their peel on, cut into pieces and seeds removed
- 3 cups self-rising flour
- 1 pinch salt
- 15 grams poppy seeds, plus extra for sprinkling
- Juice of half a lemon
- 200 grams glass or caster sugar

Tools:

- Butter or vegetable spray
- Food processor fitted with the blade attachment, or a blender
- Juicer
- Kitchen scale
- Measuring cups and spoons
- Mixing bowl
- Parchment paper
- Prep bowl
- Round pudding mold
- Sieve
- Small whisk
- Spatula

Instructions:

1.   Preheat the oven to 160–180°C / 320–356°F.

2.   Prepare the round pudding mold with oil, butter, or vegetable spray and flour.

3.   Process the sugar, oil, eggs, and the mandarin oranges.

4.   In a mixing bowl, sift the flour with a pinch of salt. Add to the food processor in 3 stages, processing between each.

5.   Transfer back to the mixing bowl, add the poppy seeds, and stir with a spatula.

6.   Place in the prepared round pudding mold.

7.   Bake for 45 minutes, more or less according to your oven.

8.   If needed, halfway through the baking, place a sheet of parchment paper on the surface of the pudding. This will ensure that it cooks well on the inside without browning on the surface.

9. In the meantime, squeeze the lemon into a small prep bowl. Whisk the juice with the icing sugar until a paste is formed.

10. Once the pudding is cooked, remove from the oven.

11. Pour the sugar-lemon paste on top and sprinkle on more poppy seeds to taste.

VERO NAJMIAS is an Argentine of Sephardic origin from Izimir, Turkey. Ever since she was a child, she cooked alongside the best: the women of her family. Vero worked in the world of advertising, radio, and TV as an announcer, dubbing artist, and host. For the past ten years she has been passionately dedicated to teaching, cooking, and maintaining the gastronomic cultural tradition of her ancestors.

BLUEBERRY PEACH DROP SCONES

Contributed by David Brotsky

PREP TIME: 15 minutes | **COOK TIME:** 15–18 minutes
TOTAL TIME: 35 minutes | **YIELD:** 8 drop scones

A cross between a scone and a drop biscuit, this recipe was inspired by a *New York Times* recipe. Scones are a traditional Scottish recipe and biscuits, often associated with American Southern cooking, emerged in the United States before the Civil War.

My mother cooked, baked, and loved to host. She had food ready for any guest who dropped by. The apple doesn't fall far from the tree; I host and "mother" my guests with food. This drop scone recipe is a favorite to bake.

The fruit gives just the right balance of sweet and savory, making these a delicious treat for breakfast, or any time. Vegan and light and fluffy with a craggy texture, they are easy to make and come together quickly in a single bowl. Avoid overmixing to keep them soft.

TIPS:

- Use 8 ounces of a single fruit.
- Swap in any fresh berries or stone fruits you like. You want about 1 ½ to 2 cups of fruit in total.
- Make sure the margarine is cold, which helps the exterior texture be more flaky.
- The recipe can easily be doubled and freezes well.

Ingredients:

- 1 ½ cups (190 grams) all-purpose flour
- 1 ounce (30 grams) granulated sugar
- 1 ½ teaspoons baking powder
- 6 tablespoons (85 grams) cold salted margarine (preferably Earth Balance brand), cut into small pea-sized cubes
- 4 ounces (125 grams) blueberries, washed and patted dry
- 4 ounces (125 grams) peaches or other stone fruit, diced
- 60 grams plant-based yogurt (or butter-milk, see tip below)

Tools:

- Bowl
- Cutting board
- Handheld pastry blender (a.k.a. pastry cutter or dough blender)
- Knife
- Mixing spoon
- Sheet pan lined with Silpat®, parchment paper, or aluminum foil
- Spoon
- Wire cooling rack (optional)

Instructions:

1. Preheat the oven to 425°F / 220°C and prepare a sheet pan with a non-stick liner.
2. In the bowl, use a spoon to mix the flour, sugar, and baking powder together. Add the margarine into the flour mixture, making sure to coat the pieces with the flour. Using a pastry blender or your fingers, work the margarine into the flour for a minute or two so they become more of a crumbly mixture. This helps ensure that the biscuits will be a bit flaky.

3. Add the fruit to the bowl and mix gently with a spoon. Make a well in the center and add yogurt or buttermilk. Stir the mixture several times until it forms an even, cohesive, and wet dough. Make sure not to overmix, but if it's still too dry to work with, add 1 or 2 teaspoons of water to ensure all the flour is mixed in and hydrated.

4. Using a spoon, drop 8 evenly sized mounds (each about a generous ¼ cup) onto the baking sheet, making sure each mound is together and a little flattened, leaving at least 1 inch between each.

5. Place the baking sheet into the preheated oven. Bake until golden brown, 15–18 minutes depending on your oven. Remove the sheet from the oven and let cool for 10 minutes on the tray or a wire rack. Serve warm or at room temperature.

> **TIP:** To use buttermilk in place of the yogurt, pour 2 ounces / 60 grams of any plant-based milk into a cup, add 1 teaspoon of vinegar, then stir and let sit so it sours and curdles a bit.

DAVID BROTSKY likes to cook, bake, and entertain his friends when he is not hiking or spending time outdoors. A lawyer who also runs Davetrek Adventures, an outdoors social group in the NY area, David has done two round-the-world trips, one just as the pandemic was breaking out in February 2020. You can follow more of his adventures on his website davetrek.com.

BOULOU BREAD WITH ORANGE, NUTS, SEEDS, AND RAISINS

Contributed by Brad Mahlof

PREP TIME: 90 minutes | **COOK TIME:** 50 minutes
TOTAL TIME: 2 hours 20 minutes | **YIELD:** 4 medium-size loaves

Boulou is an enriched bread that both Libyan and Tunisian Jews have traditionally enjoyed to break their Yom Kippur fast. The Tunisians prepare their Boulou more like a cookie leavened with baking powder; the Libyan version is more bread-like and made using yeast.

This delicious Libyan bread recipe is flavored with orange, dried fruits, and nuts and is the perfect first bite to conclude the 25-hour Yom Kippur fast. My family would traditionally enjoy Boulou with some mint tea or lemonade.

Ingredients:

For the yeast mixture:
- 1 ½ tablespoons dry yeast
- 1 teaspoon sugar
- ¼ cup water

For the dough:
- 500 grams flour
- 1 cup sugar
- 1 cup light-colored raisins soaked in warm water and drained
- ½ cup finely chopped walnuts
- ½ cup chopped almonds
- 1 ½ tablespoons whole anise seeds
- 1 ½ tablespoons nigella seeds
- 1 tablespoon sesame seeds, plus more for topping

- 2 eggs
- 1 egg yolk
- 1 pinch salt
- 1 teaspoon vanilla extract
- Lemon zest
- Orange zest
- ¾ cup water
- ¼ cup orange juice
- ¼ cup vegetable oil

For the egg wash:
- 1 egg yolk
- Sesame seeds

BRAD MAHLOF is a passionate cook and recipe creator from NYC, who cooks and bakes food that honors his Sephardi and Ashkenazi Jewish roots. Brad is the winner of PBS's *The Great American Recipe*, and his recipes have been featured in various publications. Brad loves hosting Shabbat dinners that showcase his Libyan, Israeli, and Ashkenazi recipes. He shares his passion for cooking on Instagram @cookwithbrad.

Tools:

- Baking sheet
- Kitchen scale
- Large bowl
- Measuring cups and spoons
- Mortar and pestle
- Pastry brush
- Plastic wrap

- Sharp knife
- Small prep bowl
- Spoon
- Towel
- Wooden spoon or spatula
- Zester

Instructions:

Prepare the dough:

1. Crumble the yeast in a small prep bowl or glass, add the sugar and warm water, stir, and set aside for a few minutes to activate.

2. Add the flour, sugar, raisins, walnuts, and almonds to a bowl. Mix with a wooden spoon or spatula to combine.

3. Use a mortar and pestle to slightly open up the anise seeds before adding them to the flour mixture, along with all the other dough ingredients except the oil. Mix to just combine, then leave to sit for 1–2 minutes.

4. Next, gradually add the oil and process the dough by hand into a smooth ball. Cover the dough with plastic wrap and a towel. Let the dough rest for about 40 minutes.

Shape and bake the dough:

1. On a clean work surface, divide the rested dough in half and use your hands to shape them into two oblong loaves.

2. Place the loaves on a baking sheet. Cover once again with plastic wrap and a towel on top. Let the dough rise for another 40 minutes.

3. Make shallow diagonal slits across each loaf of dough, brush with egg yolk, and sprinkle generously with sesame seeds.

4. Bake at 350°F for 50 minutes or until the Boulou is golden.

CARDAMOM HONEY COOKIES

Contributed by Donna Anavian

PREP TIME: 50 minutes | COOK TIME: 10 minutes
TOTAL TIME: 1 hour | YIELD: 24 small cookies

These Rosh Hashanah stamped cookies are based on a honey shortbread (an eggless cookie). I made this recipe with freshly ground cardamom to enhance the flavor, since I grew up in a Persian household and love the flavor. These cookies can be made with honey-themed cookie cutters with plunger stamps, or in simple circle shapes—both will delight! They have a rich honey flavor, a spicy and floral sweetness from the cardamom, and the crisp chew of a sugar cookie. Enjoy with tea!

Ingredients:

- ½ cup margarine (1 stick), salted (if unsalted, add a ¼ teaspoon of salt)
- ⅓ cup shortening
- ⅓ cup brown sugar (packed)
- ⅓ cup honey
- ¾ teaspoon finely ground cardamom (for maximum flavor, grind cardamom seeds, not the green pods, in a spice grinder or with a mortar and pestle.)
- ¼ teaspoon cinnamon
- ½ teaspoon orange blossom water (optional)
- ½ teaspoon vanilla
- ½ teaspoon baking powder
- 2 cups flour
- ⅓ cup cornstarch

Tools:

- Baking sheet
- Cookie cutters with plunger stamps in the shapes of honey jars, bees, and honeycomb (or a simple round cutter or the rim of a mug)
- Measuring cups and spoons
- Mixing bowl
- Mortar and pestle or spice grinder (optional)
- Parchment paper
- Plastic wrap
- Rolling pin
- Stand mixer or hand mixer
- Wooden spoon

Instructions:

1. In the bowl of a mixer, cream the margarine, shortening, brown sugar, and honey for 2 minutes on high speed. Prepare the cardamom and add it along with the cinnamon, orange blossom water, and vanilla and mix until blended.

2. In another bowl, mix together the flour, cornstarch, and baking powder with a wooden spoon.

3. Add the wet ingredients to the dry and mix on low speed until just blended. The mixture should come together and be like a sugar cookie dough with a very soft cloud-like texture. It should not be sticky. If the dough is too sticky, you can add up to ½ cup flour. Keep in mind that the dough will firm up a bit in the refrigerator.

4. Wrap the dough and refrigerate it for 30 minutes.

5. Meanwhile preheat the oven to 350°F / 180°C.

6. Roll out the cookie dough between two sheets of parchment paper to 6-milimeter (¼-inch) thick.

7. Cut out cookies. You can use shaped cookie cutters with imprint stamps, a simple round cutter, or the rim of a mug. Place the cut out cookies on a lined baking sheet.

8. Bake for 10 minutes or until cookies are just golden at the edges.

> **TIP:** Use a rolling pin with thickness rings—it's my favorite baking tool! It keeps the cookies even so they look beautiful and bake evenly. Plus, it makes rolling Chanukah cookies and hamantaschen a breeze!

DONNA ANAVIAN is a self-taught home baker based in NY who creates tasty recipes with artistic designs for her baking business. Her baking inspirations are the *Great British Baking Show* and her mother, who taught her all the basics. She shares her work on Instagram @donnasbakingpalette.

CHALLAH DONUTS

Contributed by Eliran Sobel

PREP TIME: 45 minutes, plus rising time (2 hours or overnight)

COOK TIME: 35 minutes | **TOTAL TIME:** 1 hour 20 minutes, plus rising time

YIELD: 12 donuts or 2 challahs

Since going vegan, I didn't want to sacrifice quality when vegan-izing the Jewish foods I grew up with. I developed a vegan challah recipe, tweaking every variable until I perfected it. Every year, my family would host a Chanukah party and make homemade donuts. I realized that my challah dough would also work for donuts, so I now use the same dough for both. As challah it's not overly sweet, and the donuts aren't overly bready once you add toppings. Non-vegan friends have said this recipe made the best challah/donuts they've had, vegan or not!

Ingredients:

- 15 grams (2 tablespoons) ground flaxseed (I use golden since I like the color better, but any ground flaxseeds will work)
- 85 grams (⅓ cup) water
- 225 grams (¾ cup + 3 tablespoons) water
- 500 grams (4–4 ½ cups) bread flour*
- 75 grams (6 tablespoons) sugar
- 60 grams (¼ cup) neutral oil, such as canola
- 10 grams (3 ¼ teaspoons) dried yeast
- 10 grams (1 ½ teaspoons) table salt
- 1+ liter (4 ½+ cups) oil for frying

Optional toppings:
- Cinnamon sugar
- Store-bought vegan frosting
- Melted chocolate chips
- Sprinkles

NOTE: Alternatively, use 470 grams (3¾–4¼ cups) all-purpose flour plus 30 grams (¼ cup) vital wheat gluten. The dough will be a bit stickier and won't rise quite as well.

Tools:

- Baking sheets or loaf tins
- Heat-safe spatula, spoon, or tongs for flipping donuts in oil
- Kitchen scale
- Large bowl, bread machine, or stand mixer with a dough hook
- Measuring cups and spoons
- Non-stick cooking spray
- Paper towels

- Parchment paper
- Plastic spatula or bench scraper
- Plates
- Spoon
- Tea towel, plastic bag, or sealable container
- Wok, dutch oven, or large pot for frying

Instructions:

Make the dough:

1. Mix the flaxseed and 85 grams (⅓ cup) water with a spoon in a large bowl, bowl of stand mixer, or bread machine basket and let sit for 5 minutes.

2. Add the remaining ingredients, except the oil for frying. If using a bread machine, set to the dough setting. Otherwise, knead for 10 minutes, either by hand or using the dough hook on a stand mixer. If kneading by hand, periodically use a bench scraper or plastic spatula to gather the dough back together. The dough should still be a bit sticky (even stickier if kneaded by hand) but come together and be more elastic than before.

3. Let the dough rise in a bowl covered with a tea towel for a minimum of 2 hours. Even better, place it in a plastic bag or sealable container and let rise overnight or up to 2 days in the fridge.

Make the donuts:

1. Divide the dough into 12 equal pieces, about 75 grams each.

2. Grease your hands with oil to make it easier to shape the sticky dough. Stretch and fold each piece in your hand to form a tight ball. Press down with your thumb to form a hole in the center and roll between your thumb and index finger to widen the hole. Make the hole bigger than you want it to end up because it will close up as it fries.

3. Place the donuts on a piece of parchment paper greased with non-stick spray and leave to rise for 1 hour. The donuts will look very small but grow a lot in the fryer.

4. Fill a large pot about halfway with oil (I like to use a wok) and heat to 350 F / 180 C. As you fry, continue to monitor the temperature, turning the heat up or down accordingly, to keep the temperature stable.

5. Fry the donuts for 1 ½–2 minutes per side until golden brown, then drain on a baking sheet lined with paper towels and dab off the excess oil. Be careful when dealing with hot oil!

6. Decorate donuts with cinnamon sugar, frosting, sprinkles, chocolate, or whatever you like! Warning: frosting will likely melt if the donuts are still hot, but the mess is part of the fun.

To make challahs:

1. Divide the dough in half to make 2 challahs. Use your favorite braiding method by following an online tutorial, or simply form into a ball or loaf as I often do.

2. Place the challahs on a baking sheet or in a loaf tin and let rise for at least an hour.

3. Bake the challahs in an oven preheated to 375°F / 190°C. Check them after 20 minutes, but they could need up to 30 minutes. They should be a pale golden color on top.

4. סע געזונטערהייט 'Es gezunterheyt'! (Yiddish for "Eat in good health!")

ELIRAN SOBEL is currently a rabbinical student at Yeshivat Chovevei Torah. A 2020 Rutgers University graduate with a degree in linguistics, he is passionate about studying and teaching Jewish text. He became vegan in 2013 and combines his passion for Jewish life and vegan cooking by veganizing his favorite Jewish foods.

CHOCOLATE CHIP BOULOU COOKIES

Contributed by Ariane Zenker

PREP TIME: 5 minutes | **COOK TIME:** 12–20 minutes
TOTAL TIME: 17–25 minutes | **YIELD:** 3–4 boulous (logs) or approximately 20 cookies

Inspired by the Sephardic Tunisian recipe, boulous are cookies traditionally made with almonds and raisins which I have replaced here with chocolate chips, while keeping the orange blossom flavor.

Baked in small round cookies (the children's favorite version) or in a small log and sliced (my favorite version), this recipe is of amazing simplicity. Not too sweet, not too fatty, pareve, prepared in 5 minutes. You should always have boulous in your cookie jar! Dip them in an orgeat syrup or a lemonade (as per the tradition), or boulous go perfectly with coffee and tea. The boulou can become your madeleine.

Ingredients:

- 100 grams vegetable oil
- 100 grams freshly squeezed orange juice (about 1 orange)
- 100 grams of sugar
- 2 large eggs (about 55 grams each)
- 1 teaspoon orange blossom water
- 500 grams flour
- 20 grams baking powder
- 5 grams salt
- 150 grams chocolate chips (swap for almonds, hazelnuts, raisins, dry fruits, or anything you like)
- Sesame seeds and/or sprinkles for decoration

Tools:

- Baking tray
- Bowl
- Kitchen scale
- Knife (optional, for logs)
- Measuring cups and spoons
- Parchment paper
- Spatula
- Stand mixer with beater tools

Instructions:

1. Preheat your oven to 160°C.

2. Pour the oil, orange juice, sugar, eggs, and orange blossom water into the bowl of a mixer. Beat for one minute at medium speed.

3. Add flour, baking powder, and salt. Beat for 30 seconds on medium speed and 10 seconds on high speed.

4. Add chocolate chips and beat for 15 seconds. Note: do not overbeat with the mixer as your dough could become hard and brownish from the melting chocolate.

5. Shaping the boulous: note that the dough should be very slightly sticky and allow you to shape between your hands easily. Add a little flour if too sticky.

6. For the small cookie-shaped version: Moisten your hands to prevent the dough from sticking. Make small balls of about 30 grams in weight and 4 centimeters in diameter. Place them on a baking tray lined with parchment paper. Flatten them with your index finger and sprinkle with sesame seeds and/or sprinkles.

7. For the original log shape: Make 18cm long and 8cm wide sausages (about 300 grams each). Sprinkle with sesame seeds.

8. Bake 12 minutes for cookies or 18–20 minutes for logs.

9. When cooked, cut the log into slices. Optional: put the slices back in the oven for 5 minutes to have more of a dry biscuit texture.

ARIANE ZENKER was raised in a Franco-British culture and introduced to pastry by her Ashkenazi grandmother. Married to an American and a mother of four children, English and "cakes" have become the language of everyday life. She created The Cake Shop in Grenoble, France, a pastry shop-boutique-workshop specializing in Anglo-Saxon pastries and cake design. Ariane believes in the benefits of everyday simple and delicious baking.

CHOCOLATE PUDDING
WITH ESPRESSO CUSTARD

Contributed by Denise Phillips

PREP TIME: 40 minutes | **COOK TIME:** 50 minutes
TOTAL TIME: 1 hour 30 minutes | **YIELD:** 8 servings

A dessert crested for anyone who loves chocolate. The recipe works if you double it and make into a large pudding or serve in individual ramekins. It is a perfect winter entertaining dessert with a great combination of coffee and chocolate—heaven on a plate!

Ingredients:

For the espresso custard:
- 125 milliliters non-dairy cream or double cream
- 125 milliliters soya milk or whole milk
- 2 eggs
- 25 grams sugar
- 1 ½ tablespoons custard powder
- 50 milliliters espresso coffee

For the chocolate pudding:
- 200 grams type 00 flour or plain white flour

- 200 grams sugar
- Pinch salt
- 2 heaped teaspoons bicarbonate soda
- 4 eggs
- 50 grams margarine or unsalted butter, melted, plus extra to grease the tin
- 60 grams smooth apricot jam
- 2 tablespoons red wine vinegar
- 160 milliliters soya milk or soya cream
- 100 grams dark chocolate, cut into chunks, or use chocolate drops

Tools:

- Baking paper or spray
- Kitchen scale
- Measuring cups and spoons
- Saucepan
- Sieve

- Spatula
- Square 1 liter tin, or 8 ramekins
- Stand mixer with whisk attachment
- Whisk

Instructions:

1. Preheat the oven to 200°C / 180°C Fan / Gas Mark 6.

2. Line and grease a 1-liter square tin or 8 ramekins.

3. For the coffee custard, heat the cream and milk together in a saucepan until almost boiling, then set aside.

4. Whisk the eggs with the sugar in a mixer then add the custard powder, followed by the cream mixture. Transfer back to the saucepan and heat gently until thickened. Stir in the espresso and set aside.

5. For the sponge, sift all the dry ingredients together, then add the eggs, melted butter, jam, and vinegar.

6. Gently beat together, then add milk and stir well. Transfer to your prepared tin or ramekins.

7. Bake for 20 minutes, remove, then gently stud the sponge with chocolate chunks. Return to the oven for a final 20 minutes.

8. Remove from the oven and set aside.

9. Cut into squares or remove from the ramekins.

10. To serve, preheat the oven to 220°C / Gas Mark 7. Put the sponge squares on a baking tray for 5 minutes.

11. Gently warm the custard and serve each pudding with custard poured over.

DENISE PHILLIPS is author of seven kosher cookbooks blending traditional and modern Jewish cooking. Her hands-on masterclasses and Zoom cookery classes provide inspiration and new skills. Denise runs "Date On A Plate" online events for singles to network and meet new people, corporate events suitable for entertaining company clients, and offers team building through cookery classes.

CINNAMON TEFF BUNDT CAKE

Contributed by Ilanit Tagaya

PREP TIME: 10 minutes │ **COOK TIME:** 40 minutes
TOTAL TIME: 50 minutes │ **YIELD:** 1 bundt cake, serves 10–15

My mother-in-law bought me one kilogram of teff flour and told me to use it for something sweet. I did several trials with this hard gluten-free flour, until finally I made this cake that turned out perfect! The star of this recipe is teff (Eragrostis tef). Teff is a tiny ancient grain native to Ethiopia and is used to make injera, a traditional Ethiopian flatbread.

Teff flour gives this cake a subtle nuttiness, perfectly paired with the comforting warmth of cinnamon. A burst of citrusy brightness comes from the addition of orange juice, while shredded coconut adds a delightful chewiness. Topped with a dusting of powdered sugar, each bite of this bundt cake is a moist and flavorful treat.

Ingredients:

- 2 cups teff flour
- 2 teaspoons baking powder
- 1 teaspoon cinnamon
- ¼ cup shredded dried coconut
- 4 eggs
- ¾ cup sugar
- 1 cup of orange juice
- ¾ cup vegetable oil
- 1 teaspoon vanilla extract
- Powdered sugar, for garnish

Tools:

- Measuring cups and spoons
- Medium bundt cake pan
- Prep bowl
- Sieve
- Stand mixer or hand mixer
- Toothpick

Instructions:

1. Preheat the oven to 170°C.
2. In a prep bowl, sift and mix dry ingredients, set aside.
3. In a stand mixer, beat the eggs, adding sugar gradually while beating for 3 minutes.
4. Reduce the mixing intensity, gradually add the orange juice, oil, and vanilla extract.
5. Fold in the dry ingredients, mixing gently for a uniform texture.
6. Pour into a greased bundt cake pan.
7. Bake for 40 minutes or until a toothpick comes out dry.
8. Allow to cool and then sprinkle with powdered sugar before serving.

ILANIT TAGAYA is an Israeli Ethiopian graphic designer residing in Israel. She loves design and baking. You can follow her creative journey on TikTok @lilush_style and discover her beautiful baking creations on Instagram @Ilanit_tag.

FRESH FRUIT DREIDELS

Contributed by Tiffany Nechama

PREP TIME: 10 minutes | **COOK TIME:** 0 minutes
TOTAL TIME: 10 minutes | **YIELD:** 6 dreidels

As the mother of two young children, I always look forward to bonding with my children through snack activities (i.e., snack-tivity). Fresh fruit dreidels teach my children about Hanukkah, and making them by themselves from start to finish gives them a sense of accomplishment. Using just bananas, strawberries, pretzel sticks, a toothpick, and optional melted chocolate, my children are able to use kid-safe knives to slice their fruit and assemble their fruit dreidels on their own. The best part about this recipe is that once the snack is put together, the fruit dreidel actually spins! My children are always giddy when they're able to play games with their food. A fun activity and snack in one!

Ingredients:

- 1 banana, peeled
- 6 strawberries, washed
- 6 mini pretzel sticks
- 1 toothpick
- Optional: ½ teaspoon coconut oil melted with ½ cup chocolate chips

Tools:

- Cutting board
- Kid-safe knives
- Small bowl and spoon
- Toothpick

Instructions:

1. Place your banana on a cutting board and slice into 1-inch coins.
2. Take your strawberries and slice off the green stems.
3. Line up a banana coin on top of a strawberry bottom.
4. Take a pretzel stick and press it down into the center of your banana slice until it pokes a hole through the bottom and into the strawberry, holding them all together.
5. Carve Hebrew letters into the banana with a toothpick.
6. If using melted chocolate, go over your carved Hebrew letters with the melted chocolate, using the toothpick like a paintbrush.
7. Spin your fruit dreidel and enjoy!

TIFFANY NECHAMA runs the blog and Instagram account @LivLaughCook, aiming to motivate others to eat healthier meals and live well-balanced lifestyles. She has been cooking with her children, Liv and Sawyer, since they were very young. Tiffany believes involving children in creating recipes, whether measuring and mixing, or growing and picking vegetables, makes them excited about trying new wholesome foods.

GRANDMA SOPHIE'S APPLE STRUDEL

Contributed by Michael Leventhal

PREP TIME: 20 minutes | **COOK TIME:** 30–35 minutes
TOTAL TIME: 55 minutes | **YIELD:** 8–10 servings

For many years, Shabbat at my house was only complete with two rolls of my Grandma Sophie's perfect, freshly made apple strudel. They were eagerly awaited, arrived every Friday afternoon in a plastic box, and were devoured by Sunday morning. Grandma insisted we eat everything quickly while the pastry was still fresh. The same crooked plastic box was returned so it could be refilled the following week. My Grandma made strudel well into her nineties. She would have been flattered—but mostly bemused and surprised—to see her recipe here in such good company!

Ingredients:

- Plain (all-purpose) flour for dusting the work surface
- 375 grams (14 ounces) filo pastry, thawed
- 1 tablespoon vegetable oil
- 8 tablespoons good raspberry jam
- 4 tablespoons ground almonds
- 4 medium Bramley cooking apples
- 170 grams (6 ounces / ¾ cup) raisins or sultanas
- ½ teaspoon ground cinnamon
- 1 medium egg, beaten
- Icing sugar for dusting

Tools:

- Baking tray
- Colander
- Cutting board
- Grater
- Kitchen scale
- Measuring spoons
- Palette knife
- Parchment paper
- Pastry brush
- Sharp knife
- Small sieve for dusting icing sugar
- Vegetable peeler
- Whisk

Instructions:

1. Preheat the oven to 180°C / 350°F / Gas Mark 4.
2. Dust your work surface with flour. Cut the entire packet of filo sheets in half widthways. Each half should be a rectangle of about 30cm x 40cm (11" x 15").
3. Place one sheet on a lightly floured surface or a large piece of parchment paper.
4. Lightly brush the pastry with half of the oil, leaving a 2.5-centimeter (1-inch) clean border.
5. Using a palette knife, spread 4 tablespoons of the jam in an even layer within the border and sprinkle 2 tablespoons of ground almonds on top.
6. Peel, core, and grate the apples. Place in a colander and squeeze out as much juice as you can. Spread half the amount over the pastry in an even layer. Sprinkle half of the raisins or sultanas and add a pinch of cinnamon.
7. Roll the longest edge of the pastry to form a log and carefully transfer to a baking tray lined with parchment paper, making sure the seal is facing down. Tuck the ends of the filo dough under at the ends.
8. Brush the strudel surface with the beaten egg.

9.   Repeat all the steps above to make a second strudel.

10.   Bake until the strudel is golden and puffed. It should take about 30–35 minutes.

11.   Carefully, by lifting up the parchment paper, transfer the strudel to a wire rack to cool.

12.   Once the strudels are cooled, dust the top with icing sugar using a sieve, and cut into slices.

13.   Eat quickly, before the pastry gets sad.

14.   Repeat next week.

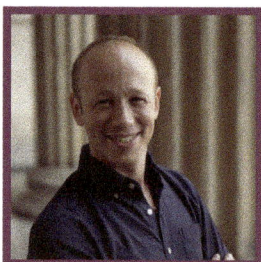

MICHAEL LEVENTHAL is a writer, editor, and publisher. He edited the *Jewish Quarterly* journal, co-authored *Jews in Britain*, authored the children's book *The Chocolate King*, and compiled a fundraising cookbook of Jewish chocolate recipes called *Babka, Boulou & Blintzes*. He is the founder of the food charity Gefiltefest and still spends too much time thinking about food and eating chocolate.

GREIBES: ALMOND BUTTER COOKIES

Contributed by Nelson Wejkin

PREP TIME: 20 minutes | **COOK TIME**: 10 minutes
TOTAL TIME: 30 minutes | **YIELD**: 40 cookies

Greibes are a typical recipe of the Jewish community of Syria and Lebanon that I make in Argentina. In the sweet recipes from these communities, almonds and orange water are favorite ingredients. This recipe calls for 0000 flour, which is simply highly refined flour that is whiter in color and has little gluten formation. It is only used for breads and pastry recipes. If you can't find it, you can use a pizza flour from the supermarket.

Ingredients:

- 300 grams 0000 flour
- 100 grams icing sugar
- 200 grams margarine
- 1 teaspoon orange blossom water
- 100 grams blanched almonds
- Powdered sugar to sprinkle

Tools:

- Baking sheet
- Cutting board
- Kitchen scale
- Large mixing bowl
- Measuring cups and spoons
- Sharp knife
- Sieve
- Spatula or wooden spoon

Instructions:

1. Preheat oven 300°F / 150°C.
2. Mix the sieved flour with the icing sugar using a spatula or wooden spoon in a large mixing bowl.
3. Add the cold margarine, cut into cubes, combining to form a sand-like texture.
4. Add the orange blossom water and combine everything.

5.   Make small balls and place them on a clean baking sheet.

6.   Squash each slightly, and place a whole almond in the center.

7.   Bake in a warm oven for 10 minutes, until they are cooked but haven't browned.

8.   Sprinkle with powdered sugar before serving.

NELSON WEJKIN is a chef, cooking teacher, and specialist in Jewish cuisine. He gives Jewish cookery classes in communities in Argentina and neighboring countries. Nelson is in charge of the kitchen on the Argentinian public television show, *Shalom Amia*.

HALVA WITH VANILLA AND PISTACHIO

Contributed by The Jewish Food Hero Kitchen

PREP TIME: 10 minutes, plus 2 hours cooling time | **COOK TIME:** 0 minutes
TOTAL TIME: 2 hours 10 minutes | **YIELD:** 1 block of halva or 20–25 pieces

This pistachio and vanilla halva recipe is designed with home cooks in mind: no candy thermometer needed. The recipe is full of flavor and easy to prepare. Adding coconut flour makes the halva set nicely and gives it a soft but still crumbly texture. I prefer this halva recipe to most professionally produced versions—it's just sweet enough, and full of protein and fiber from the tahini and coconut flour.

Ingredients:

- 1 cup runny tahini (sesame paste)
- ¼ cup honey
- 2 tablespoons vanilla extract
- ¾ cup fine coconut flour
- Coconut oil (optional)
- ¼ teaspoon salt
- ¼ cup shelled pistachios, roughly chopped

Tools:

- Loaf pan or a container to set the halva
- Measuring cups and spoons
- Medium bowl
- Parchment paper
- Spatula

HERE ARE SOME FLAVOR ADAPTATIONS:

- Replace the pistachios with sliced almonds or walnuts.
- Swap the vanilla for instant coffee.
- Make a marbled halva by stirring a couple tablespoons of cocoa powder into half of the base before swirling both parts together.

Instructions:

1. In a medium bowl, combine the tahini, honey, and vanilla extract with a spatula. Mix until mostly smooth—the mixture will become thick.

2. Slowly add in the coconut flour, a couple tablespoons at a time, until you get a very smooth and thick dough. Depending on how runny your tahini is, you might need to use a couple tablespoons less or more of coconut oil.

3. Stir in the salt and the pistachios.

4. Line a loaf pan or a container with parchment paper on all sides. Transfer the halva to the parchment-lined container and press it down really well using a spatula or your hands. Line the top of the halva with a piece of parchment paper and compress it as best as you can. Place the halva in the fridge to set for at least 2 hours.

5. Remove the halva from the fridge and slice as desired.

From The Jewish Food Hero Kitchen

HUSHQUILIQ:
BUKHARIAN COILED FRIED COOKIES

Contributed by Manashe Khaimov

PREP TIME: 30 minutes, plus 1 hour for rising
COOK TIME: 2–3 minutes per batch | **TOTAL TIME:** 1 hour 45 minutes
YIELD: 25–35 coiled dough treats, depending on the size of each piece of dough

Hushquiliq is a traditional fried Hanukkah dessert that originates from the Bukharian Jewish community, particularly from Central Asia, including Uzbekistan. It's a coiled fried cookie that bears a resemblance to a loosely scrolled piece of parchment that is enjoyed during Hanukkah.

The recipe involves rolling out the dough into thin strips, coiling them, and then frying them until they achieve a golden-brown color. The use of oil in frying is a symbolic nod to the miracle of the oil found by the Maccabees when they reclaimed the Temple in Jerusalem, a central theme in Hanukkah celebrations.

This recipe for coiled fried cookies is adapted from Amnun Kimyagarov's book *Classic Central Asian (Bukharian) Jewish Cuisine and Custom* (2010).

Ingredients:

- ½ teaspoon baking soda
- 2 tablespoons vodka
- 8 eggs
- Pinch of salt
- 2 teaspoons sugar
- ⅜ cup of warm water
- 7 ¼ cups flour
- 1 ⅔ cups vegetable oil (for frying)
- 2 tablespoons confectioners' sugar, to garnish before serving

Tools:

- Colander
- Dutch oven or deep saucepan
- Mixing bowl
- Paper towels
- Rolling pin
- Sharp knife

- Skimmer spoon (to remove fried cookies from cooking oil)
- Small sieve for dusting icing
- Towel
- Wooden spoon or spatula

Instructions:

1. In a mixing bowl, dissolve the baking soda in vodka.
2. Add eggs, salt, sugar, and cup of warm water. Stir and beat well with a wooden spoon or spatula.
3. Add the flour and mix. The dough should be stiff. If it's not, add a little more flour.
4. Cover the bowl with a towel and let the dough rest for one hour.
5. Divide the dough into 25–35 pieces (depending on how big you make the coils) and shape them into balls.
6. Set the oil in a Dutch oven or deep saucepan and allow it to heat while you shape the dough. For deep frying, you want the oil to reach a temperature between 350–375°F / 175–190°C to ensure quick and even cooking without becoming too oily.
7. Work with each ball of dough individually from start to frying before moving on to the next ball.
8. Take one of the balls and roll it out into a rectangle. Note that due to the stiffness of the dough, rolling may be difficult and requires patience. It's essential for the final cooking and texture that the dough be as thin as possible and completely dry. If it's not dry, dust the dough with extra flour.
9. Cut the rectangle into strips slightly larger than ½-inch wide.
10. Shape the strips into coils so they resemble loosely scrolled pieces of parchment: slightly spread apart the index and middle finger on your non-dominant hand. Using your dominant hand, gently wrap a strip around the open fingers. Close your fingers, remove the roll and set aside.

11. Repeat with the other strips.

12. Add the coils to the hot oil and cook until they turn golden brown. Depending on the depth of your pan, you may need to flip them once to ensure even cooking. If the rolls are too tight they won't cook properly, but too loose and they'll unravel during cooking. Test the tightness with the first few coils before proceeding with the rest of the batch.

13. Once cooked, use the skimmer spoon to place the fried coils in a single layer in a colander positioned over paper towels to allow excess oil to drain.

14. Transfer the cooled coils to a plate and proceed to roll out, shape and fry the next coil of dough.

15. Repeat the shaping and frying process for the remaining dough coils until all the coils are cooked and cooled.

16. Dust the cooled coils with powdered sugar before serving. These fried coils are best enjoyed within several hours of being prepared for optimal freshness and flavor.

MANASHE KHAIMOV is Founder and CEO of SAMi (Sephardi American Mizrahi initiative) as well as established the Bukharian Jewish Union, AskBobo.org, and The Jewish Silk Road Tours™ in NYC. Recognized as "Person of the Year" by the Bukharian Jewish Congress and "36 Under 36" by *NY Jewish Week*, Manashe is a member of the Queens Jewish Advisory Council.

ISRAELI CHOCOLATE RUGELACH

Contributed by Renana Spiegel Levkovich

PREP TIME: 15 minutes, plus 1 hour 30 minutes resting time
COOK TIME: 25 minutes | **TOTAL TIME:** 2 hours 10 minutes | **YIELD:** 16 rugelach

Israeli rugelach are made with yeast, in contrast to the cream cheese–based rugelach popular in the United States. In this recipe, I give options for three fillings: chocolate, pumpkin spice, and date with ginger and nuts. Rugelach is the perfect dessert to break the fast of Yom Kippur.

Ingredients:

For the dough:
- 3 cups (500 grams) all-purpose flour
- ¾ cup water
- ¼ cup sugar
- ¼ cup vegetable oil
- 1 tablespoon dry yeast
- 1 egg
- 1 teaspoon vanilla extract or paste
- 1 beaten egg, for the egg wash

For the chocolate filling:
- 10 tablespoons sugar
- 7 tablespoons vegetable oil
- 5 tablespoons cocoa powder

Sugar syrup:
- ½ cup sugar
- ½ cup water

Alternative fillings:
- Pumpkin filling: mix ¾ cup pumpkin puree with 1 teaspoon pumpkin pie spice and ½ cup sugar.
- Date filling: blend 20 pitted Medjool dates with ½ teaspoon ginger and 2 tablespoons orange juice. Stir through a handful of chopped walnuts.

Tools:

- Baking pan
- Cling wrap or kitchen towel
- Kitchen scale
- Measuring cups and spoons
- Pastry brush
- Pizza cutter or knife
- Prep bowls
- Rolling pin
- Small saucepan
- Stand mixer

Instructions:

1. In a stand mixer bowl, place all dough ingredients and knead for 4 minutes. If the dough is too dry and doesn't come together, add 2–3 tablespoons of water.

2. Transfer the ball of dough to a medium greased bowl. Cover with cling wrap or a kitchen towel and leave it to rise for 1 hour 30 minutes.

3. Meanwhile, in a small bowl, mix all of the chocolate filling ingredients.

4. When the dough has risen, divide it into 2 and roll out each part into a circle.

5. Spread the filling on top of one rolled circle. Place the second circle on top of the one with the filling.

6. Roll out the dough sandwich to flatten it a bit more.

7. With a pizza cutter or a knife, cut into 16 triangles. Roll each triangle from the wide part to the narrow one.

8. Place all the rugelach cookies on a baking pan. Let the rugelach rise again for 1 hour.

9. Heat the oven to 180°C / 350°F with the fan.

10. Brush the rugelach with a beaten egg wash and bake for 20–25 minutes.

11. While they bake, cook sugar and water in a small saucepan on high until all sugar is dissolved.

12. Allow both the sugar syrup and baked rugelach to cool a bit.

13. Before serving, brush with the sugar syrup.

RENANA SPIEGEL LEVKOVICH is an Israeli web development expert who is also a food blogger and food photographer. Her blog renanas.kitchen shares kosher and mostly vegetarian recipes for all the family to enjoy.

KANAVLI: SEMOLINA AND COCONUT CAKE

Contributed by Ken Daniels

PREP TIME: 20 minutes | **RESTING TIME:** 1 hour 30 minutes
COOK TIME: 40 minutes | **TOTAL TIME:** 2 hours 30 minutes | **YIELD:** 12–15 servings

Kanavli is a semolina and coconut cake for Shabbat morning. This cake is mainly prepared by the Bene Israel (Jews from India). The main ingredients are semolina and coconut and it has a very grainy texture. In the early days, preparing the cake was a long process. The flesh of the coconut was grated and—through a long and tedious process—the milk was extracted. That milk was used in many of our desserts and curries. This special recipe was handed down to my wife from my dear mother-in-law Jerusha, who originally would cook the cake in a special pot over a stove-top flame. However, now the process has been modified and, with the convenience of readily available canned coconut milk and other accessible ingredients, the cake can be effortlessly prepared with a truly wonderful result.

Ingredients:

- 1 cup fine semolina, uncooked (do not use semolina flour)
- 1 cup grated coconut, dry or desiccated
- 1 cup sugar
- 1 teaspoon ground cardamom
- ¼ teaspoon ground nutmeg
- ½ cup chopped almonds, or any other nut to your liking
- ½ cup raisins
- ½ cup melted margarine or butter
- ½ cup thick coconut milk
- 3 eggs, beaten
- 1 teaspoon pure vanilla essence
- Pinch of salt
- Powdered sugar, for serving (optional)

Tools:

- Baking pan
- Cling wrap
- Frying pan
- Large mixing bowl
- Large wooden spoon
- Measuring cups and spoons
- Parchment paper
- 9-inch square pan or 10-inch diameter-round springform pan
- Toothpick or skewer

Instructions:

1. Line your baking pan with baking paper.
2. Place semolina in a frying pan and roast over medium heat until the grains turn golden brown, mixing frequently. Allow roasted semolina to cool.
3. In a large bowl, mix the cooled semolina, grated coconut, sugar, cardamom, nutmeg, almonds, and raisins. Add melted margarine or butter, coconut milk, eggs, vanilla, and a pinch of salt and mix thoroughly until all is well combined. Cover the bowl with cling wrap and set aside to rest for 1 hour 30 minutes. This will create a textured, soft, and moist cake.
4. Towards the end of the resting time, preheat the oven to 350°F / 175°C.
5. After the 1 hour and 30 minutes has elapsed, pour the mixture into your prepared baking pan and place on the middle oven rack for 40 minutes. Oven times may vary, so check the cake by inserting a toothpick or skewer to ensure the cake is no longer wet inside. The cake should be golden brown.
6. Let the cake cool down and then remove from the pan. Serve as is or if desired, sprinkle with powdered sugar. Enjoy!

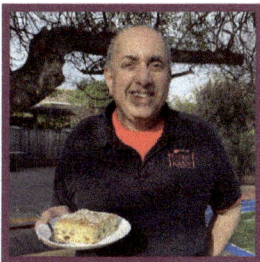

KEN DANIELS was born in Bombay. At one year old, he and his family immigrated to Newfoundland, Canada, and then to Toronto when Ken was seven. Ken now calls Australia home, having moved to Melbourne with his wife Esther and son Joshua to be closer to family. Ken and Esther manage the King David School canteens, creating wonderful food for staff and students.

KISSEL: CHILLED OAT MOUSSE

Contributed by Nelly Shulman

PREP TIME: 1 hour | **COOK TIME:** 15 minutes
TOTAL TIME: 1 hour 15 minutes, plus chilling time | **YIELD:** 100 milliliters (½ cup)

Chilled Oat Mousse is a very traditional Russian dish that my grandmother always made for me. The north of Russia, where I grew up, has almost no fruit. *Kissel*, as this dish is called in Russian, is always served with berries (in the summer) or with a jam (in winter), but, of course, you can add any fruits you'd like. It tastes great sprinkled with chopped nuts, and you can use gluten-free oats if you wish. This is a very simple recipe, but for me it evokes a lot of fond childhood memories. The quantities here are for a single serving dessert and can be scaled up for more.

Ingredients:
_____

- 50 grams (½ cup) oats
- 100 grams (½ cup) boiled water
- Optional: fruits, berries, chopped nuts

Tools:
_____

- Blender
- Bowl
- Cheesecloth
- Kitchen scale or measuring cups
- Saucepan
- Sieve
- Whisk

Instructions:
_____

1. Soak oats in chilled boiled water for an hour.
2. Blend and strain through the cheesecloth set over a sieve. Put the strained oat milk into the pan (and reserve the remaining oats to use in cookies if you want).
3. Bring the oat milk to the boil on a low heat, constantly whisking.
4. Remove from the heat and whisk into a mousse.
5. Chill and serve with fruit, berries, or nuts.

NELLY SHULMAN is a writer currently based in Berlin. Her work has appeared on JewishFiction.net, in the Vine Leaves Press Anthology of the Best 2021 Flash Fiction, and in various literary magazines. She is a winner of two writing awards. Connect with her and her work on nellyshulman.blog.

MAGIC COOKIE BARS

Contributed by Hillel Norry

PREP TIME: 15–20 minutes, plus 15 minutes cooling time | **COOK TIME:** 25 minutes
TOTAL TIME: 1 hour | **YIELD:** 20+ cookie bars

My mother often made these delicious treats for holidays and other celebrations. They were always one of my favorites. We both became vegetarian around the same time in the 1980s, and I am sure she would appreciate this vegan version of her original recipe.

Ingredients:

- ½ cup Earth Balance or other vegan butter substitute
- 1 ½ cups vegan graham cracker crumbs
- 1 cup nuts, chopped (I use pecans to celebrate our family's southern roots)

- 1 cup vegan chocolate chips
- 1 ⅓ cups shredded coconut
- 1 ⅓ cups (1 can) condensed coconut milk

Tools:

- Cake pan (not pyrex), 13" x 9" x 2"
- Cutting board
- Measuring cups and spoons
- Rubber spatula
- Sharp knife
- Small saucepan

Instructions:

1. Preheat oven to 350°F / 180°C.
2. Melt butter in a small saucepan.
3. Remove from heat and stir in graham cracker crumbs until thoroughly combined.
4. Press into the bottom of the cake pan to form the crust.
5. Add nuts, chocolate chips, and coconut one by one to form even layers.
6. Slowly pour condensed coconut milk on top so it completely covers everywhere.
7. Bake for 25 minutes.
8. Cool for 15 minutes.
9. Slice into bars.

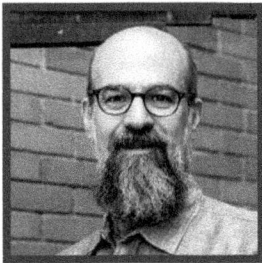

HILLEL NORRY is a rabbi in Atlanta, Georgia. He is passionate about veganism and martial arts. Hillel cherishes the recipe box he inherited from his mother, Sharon, who first taught him to cook.

MAKROUDS: SEMOLINA PASTRY WITH DATE FILLING

Contributed by Avital Cohen

PREP TIME: 5 minutes, plus 30 minutes for dough to rest | **COOK TIME:** 30 minutes
TOTAL TIME: 1 hour 5 minutes | **YIELD:** 25 makrouds

My paternal and maternal grandmothers each had their own way of making makrouds. I would always find these date cakes on Jewish holidays, alongside the traditional manicotti and yoyos. This recipe, which is very simple to make, is known throughout the Maghreb. These cakes can be fried or baked—this recipe is for baked makrouds soaked in a honey orange blossom syrup.

Ingredients:

For the semolina dough:
- 300 grams medium semolina
- 10 centiliters (100 milliliters) lukewarm water (approx. 1 glass)
- 7.5 centiliters (75 milliliters) sunflower oil (because it is a neutral oil)

For the date paste:
- 15 dates (Medjool if possible, but Deglet Nour are fine too!) or 150 grams of prepared date paste

- 10 centiliters (100 milliliters) orange blossom water
- Optional spices: 1 teaspoon ground cinnamon, or ½ teaspoon of ground cinnamon and ½ teaspoon of ground cloves

For the honey syrup:
- ½ cup honey
- 2 tablespoons orange blossom water
- Juice of 1 lemon

Tools:

- Baking sheet
- Blender
- Colander
- Kitchen scale
- Large mixing bowl

- Measuring cups and spoons
- Parchment paper
- Rolling pin
- Rubber spatula or wooden spoon
- Steamer basket set inside pressure cooker

Instructions:

1. In a large bowl, add the semolina, water, and oil. Mix everything with a rubber spatula or wooden spoon and set aside in the refrigerator for at least 30 minutes, so that the semolina swells.

2. Preheat the oven to 170°C.

3. Cook the dates in a steamer basket set inside a pressure cooker for about 20 minutes.

4. Once cooked, chop the dates in a blender with a tablespoon of orange blossom water and any optional spices you'd like to include.

5. Take the semolina dough out of the refrigerator. Split in two, and place one half back in the refrigerator until ready to use. Roll out each dough half into a rectangle, and add a strip of date dough about 2cm wide down the center. Roll the dough up and over the date filling, to form a long log. Cut slices across the width of the log, making pieces about 3cm wide (it's possible to make them wider if you'd prefer larger cakes).

6. Proceed in this way until you have used up the date paste and the dough produced from the semolina.

7. Place all the cakes on a baking sheet lined with parchment paper. Pour the remaining orange blossom water over the cakes.

8. Place in the oven for around 30 minutes. Watch carefully so that cookies are baked just until they are golden and crispy.

9. Meanwhile, make the honey syrup by placing honey, orange blossom water, and lemon juice in bowl and mixing thoroughly.

10. While still hot, dip each makroud in the sugar syrup and then place in a colander to cool down and drain.

11. When cool, place in an airtight container.

AVITAL COHEN is currently pursuing a doctorate in Biblical Studies. Originally from Tunisia, her grandparents and parents emigrated to France about fifty years ago.

MANDELBREAD WITH CHOCOLATE CHIPS

Contributed by Sarah Parkes

PREP TIME: 10 minutes | **COOK TIME:** 35 minutes
TOTAL TIME: 60 minutes, including cooling time | **YIELD:** 20 mandelbread pieces

Mandelbread is a Jewish dessert from Eastern Europe that resembles biscotti. The name "mandelbread" comes from the Yiddish word "mandelbrot," meaning "almond bread," a reference to the traditional ingredient. Every Friday afternoon, I would come home to the smell of my mom's freshly baked chocolate chip mandelbread. Once I entered adulthood, I began testing out her recipe and created a small business located in NYC called Sparkes Kitchen, focusing on giving classic mandelbread a playful, modern twist.

Ingredients:

- 3 cups (400 grams) flour
- 1 cup (200 grams) sugar
- 1 teaspoon baking powder
- Pinch of salt
- Pinch of cinnamon
- 125 grams chocolate chips
- 3 eggs
- 1 cup canola oil
- 1 teaspoon vanilla

Tools:

- Baking sheet pan
- Kitchen scale
- Knife or pastry scraper
- Large mixing bowl
- Measuring cups and spoons
- Medium mixing bowl
- Parchment paper
- Spatula
- Whisk

Instructions:

1. Set the oven to 350°F.
2. In a large bowl, combine flour, sugar, baking powder, salt, cinnamon, and chocolate chips. Whisk and set aside.
3. In a medium bowl, add 3 cracked eggs, oil, and vanilla. Whisk to combine.
4. Add the wet ingredients into the dry ingredients and mix together.
5. Separate the dough into 3 loaves on a baking sheet.
6. Bake for 20 minutes and let cool.
7. Using a knife or pastry scraper, slice loaves horizontally, in pieces about 1 inch in width. Place the pieces on their sides.
8. Return the tray to the oven for 10 minutes.
9. Once removed and cooled, flip the mandelbread pieces over to the opposite side.
10. Return the tray to the oven for 5 minutes.
11. Optional: after the mandelbread cools, cut off the sides and dip them in melted chocolate and sprinkles, nuts, etc.

SARAH PARKES is the founder of Sparkes Kitchen, a woman-owned small business that specializes in reimagining traditional Eastern European desserts. Sarah is dedicated to diversity and inclusion, and donates a portion of her profits to non-profit organizations that create meaningful job training and opportunities for individuals with disabilities.

MOLASSES GINGER COOKIES

Contributed by Debra Klein

PREP TIME: 10 minutes | **COOK TIME:** 10 minutes
TOTAL TIME: 20 minutes | **YIELD:** 20 cookies

Vegan Molasses Ginger Cookies are soft and chewy inside with perfectly crispy edges. Everyone's favorite holiday cookie takes 20 minutes to make and tastes incredible. Make a double or triple batch and stash in the freezer! These are perfect for Rosh Hashanah, break fast on Yom Kippur, Sukkot, and Hanukkah.

Ingredients:

- 1 ounce dark chocolate, finely chopped
- 1 cup all-purpose flour
- 1 teaspoon baking soda
- ½ teaspoon baking powder
- 1 teaspoon ground ginger
- 1 teaspoon cinnamon
- ¼ teaspoon ground cloves
- ¼ teaspoon sea salt
- ½ cup tahini
- ¼ cup unsulphured molasses
- 6 tablespoons pure maple syrup
- 1 teaspoon vanilla extract

Tools:

- Cutting board
- Measuring cups and spoons
- Medium-sized bowl
- Parchment paper, unbleached
- Rimmed baking sheet
- Rubber spatula
- Shallow bowl
- Sharp knife
- Small bowl
- Wire cooling rack

Instructions:

1. Preheat the oven to 350°F and line a rimmed baking sheet with unbleached parchment paper.

2. Finely chop chocolate and set aside in a shallow bowl.

3. Combine flour, baking soda, baking powder, ginger, cinnamon, cloves, and salt in a medium-sized bowl. Mix thoroughly with a spatula. You'll want to make sure baking powder is evenly distributed throughout.

4. In a small bowl, mix the wet ingredients (tahini, molasses, maple syrup, and vanilla) until well combined with a spatula.

5. Pour wet ingredients into the dry and mix until just combined.

6. Portion out cookies: Scoop 1 tablespoon of dough out and drop into the bowl of chopped chocolate.

7. Roll the cookie over so the chocolate is on top and place cookie dough onto the prepared cookie sheet. Repeat with remaining dough, leaving 2–3 inches between cookies so they have room to spread.

8. Bake for 10 minutes.

9. Let cookies cool for 5 minutes on the baking tray, so chocolate isn't so gooey, then transfer to a wire rack and allow to cool completely before storing.

10. Store at room temperature for up to a week, or in the freezer for 3 months.

TIPS:

- **Chocolate dusting:** Use coarse sugar instead of the chopped chocolate if you prefer.
- **Flour:** I used whole wheat flour. I also tested the recipe with King Arthur measure for measure gluten-free flour and they came out great. Any all-purpose flour will work, including whole wheat pastry flour. I would NOT recommend replacing the flour with almond flour; the moisture content will not be equal.
- **Tahini:** An awesome choice for oil-free and dairy-free cookies, rather than vegan butter. I adore the subtle sesame flavor the tahini imparts on these cookies, but if sesame allergies are an issue, replace the tahini with a drippy almond butter.
- **Molasses:** These are molasses cookies and their flavor and texture depends on unsulphured molasses. You could substitute additional maple syrup, but it doesn't have quite the same caramel-like flavor.
- **Maple syrup:** Pure maple syrup, either grade A or B. You can also use a lighter amber-colored syrup or a deeper colored syrup. The cookies will be a bit dark already because of the molasses.
- **Spices:** Ground ginger, cinnamon, and cloves give these cookies their gingerbread cookie taste. I love the rich, cozy spice profile and sometimes add an extra pinch of cloves as well.
- **Baking powder and soda:** This is what makes these vegan cookies rise and become soft and chewy. If you're looking for a crisper cookie, just leave the cookies in the oven a bit longer, but don't skimp on the leavening.

DEBRA KLEIN is a Holistic Health Coach and Culinary Instructor, inspiring healthy choices with seasonal plant-based recipes. She's passionate about transforming traditional Jewish foods into dishes that are nutritious, delicious, beautiful, and satisfying.

LAURENCE ORAH PHITOUSSI is a Parisian publicist. She used to order Shabbat food from good Parisian caterers. One day she realized that if she cooked for Shabbat, then the spirit of Shabbat would be in her, her kitchen, and her home. She has since written three cookbooks: *La cuisine du Shabbat en 30 minutes*, *La cuisine Shabbat Light*, and *Jewish Holiday Cooking*.

MONTECAO ALMOND SHORTBREAD

Contributed by Laurence Orah Phitoussi

PREP TIME: 10 minutes | **COOK TIME:** 25 minutes
TOTAL TIME: 35 minutes | **YIELD:** 15 pieces

These very crumbly almond powder shortbread biscuits are present in Jewish and Berber cultures, and probably originated in the Andalucia region in Southern Spain. When I was young, I dreamed of these cakes prepared by my aunts, without ever imagining that they were so easy to cook. We prepare them for all parties, and they keep well in a cake box. They are delicious with mint tea or coffee!

Ingredients:

- 200 grams flour
- 100 grams ground almonds
- 80 grams caster sugar
- 120 grams peanut oil
- 2 teaspoons cinnamon or cacao powder

Tools:

- Baking sheet
- Bowl
- Kitchen scale
- Measuring spoons
- Mixing spoon
- Parchment paper
- Small sieve for dusting

Instructions:

1. Preheat oven to 180°C / 350°F. Place parchment paper on baking sheet.
2. Mix everything except the cinnamon and knead the dough until well combined.
3. Form 15 balls.
4. Dust each ball with ground cinnamon or cocoa powder.
5. Place balls on the baking sheet.
6. Bake for 25 minutes.
7. Allow to cool at room temperature and then place in an airtight container.

PEANUT BUTTER CHOCOLATE CHIP BITES

Contributed by The Jewish Food Hero Kitchen

PREP TIME: 10 minutes | **COOK TIME:** 0 minutes
TOTAL TIME: 10 minutes | **YIELD:** 20–22 balls

Having grown up in America, peanut butter is my love language and a way of life. My grandparents never ate it, my mother is indifferent to it, and I can't imagine my life without it! These five-ingredient, gluten-free, pareve, no-bake peanut butter bites are a perfect healthy daily treat—the right portion size, satisfying with a fudge-like texture from peanut butter and coconut flour, and just the right amount of sweetness from chocolate and honey. These pareve treats are perfect to make in advance and enjoy all the time.

Ingredients:

- 1 cup peanut butter (natural, smooth, and drippy)
- 2 tablespoons honey (or agave nectar for a vegan version)
- ½ teaspoon vanilla extract
- ½ cup fine coconut flour
- Pinch of salt
- ½ cup mini dark chocolate chips (optional)

Tools:

- Measuring cups and spoons
- Medium mixing bowl
- Parchment paper
- Rimmed baking sheet, large
- Rubber spatula
- Spoon

Instructions:

1. Combine peanut butter, honey, and vanilla extract in a medium bowl and stir until smooth and creamy.
2. Add the coconut flour and salt to the bowl and mix until the coconut flour is well-incorporated and a thick and smooth cookie dough forms.
3. Stir in the chocolate chips (if using) and set the cookie dough aside for 5 minutes to allow the coconut flour to firm up further.
4. Line a rimmed baking sheet with a piece of parchment paper.
5. Scoop up a small spoonful of the peanut butter cookie dough at a time. Roll between your hands to form smooth, small balls. If the balls feel too sticky at this point, add up to ¼ cup more coconut flour to firm up the dough.
6. Transfer the balls onto the prepared baking sheet and repeat the process until you've formed around 20–22 peanut butter balls.
7. Allow to chill in the fridge for a few hours before serving. The peanut butter balls will keep in the refrigerator for at least 5–6 days.

From The Jewish Food Hero Kitchen

PIZZA EBRAICA:
CHEWY UNLEAVENED DRIED FRUIT CAKES

Contributed by Silvia Nacamulli

PREP TIME: 20 minutes, plus overnight marinating (optional) & 20 minutes cooling
COOK TIME: 15–22 minutes
TOTAL TIME: 1 hour, plus overnight marinating time (optional)
YIELD: 15–18 large or 25–28 finger-sized cakes

These fruit cakes are a unique delicacy, and one of the oldest Roman Jewish recipes. In fact, until the 19th century, the word *pizza* was used mostly for cakes, sweets, and focaccias.

Traditionally baked for family celebrations, such as weddings, bar/bat mitzvahs, and brits, Pizza Ebraica is usually given in a little sachet as a take-home present. It usually comes in large, brick-like pieces, but you can also make smaller fat-finger size portions.

Most people would buy the *Pizza* (as it is most commonly called) already made from *Boccione*, a wonderful little bakery in the main square (Piazza) of the former Roman Jewish ghetto. However, when it comes to large celebrations, in my family we enjoy baking our own. Here is our family recipe.

Ingredients:

- 100 grams (3 ½ ounces) raisins or sultanas
- 100 grams (3 ½ ounces / ⅔ cup) almonds
- 50 grams (1 ¾ ounces / scant ½ cup) pine nuts
- 200 grams (7 ounces) mixed candied fruit or glacé cherries (or a mix)
- 100 milliliters (3 ½ fluid ounces / scant ½ cup) dry white wine
- 1 teaspoon vanilla extract

- 230 milliliters (7 ½ fluid ounces / scant 1 cup) sunflower oil
- 500 grams (1 pound 2 ounces / 4 cups) plain white flour (ideally 00 type) or 350 grams (12 ounces / 2 ¼ cups) flour and
- 150 grams (5 ½ ounces / 1 ½ cups) ground almonds (for a more almondy flavor)
- 170 grams (5 ¾ ounces / ¾ cup) caster or granulated sugar
- Pinch of salt

Tools:

- Baking tray
- Chopping board
- Kitchen scale
- Large mixing bowl
- Large spoon
- Measuring jug, cups, and spoons
- Medium mixing bowl
- Parchment paper
- Sharp knife
- Small saucepan or heat-proof microwavable container
- Wire cooling rack

Instructions:

1. Place the raisins or sultanas, almonds, pine nuts, and candied fruit or glacé cherries in a medium bowl.

2. Add the wine and the vanilla extract and leave to soak while you prepare the rest of the ingredients. Tip: For a richer taste, and if you have the time, leave the fruit and nuts to soak for a few hours or overnight.

3. Heat the oil in a small saucepan over medium heat or in a microwavable container in the microwave until warm, but not hot.

4. Put the flour (or flour and ground almonds) in a large bowl, then add the warm oil and mix well with a large spoon.

5. Add the sugar and salt and mix again, this time with your hands.

6. Add the soaked nuts, candied fruit, and wine to the flour and oil mixture and mix with clean hands until everything is evenly distributed. Don't worry if it appears a little crumbly—that's quite normal.

7. On a clean surface, divide the mixture into thirds or quarters.

8. Mold each piece into long, chunky rectangular blocks.

9. Score a few long lines on the top.

10. Use a sharp knife to cut each block into five or six brick-type blocks, roughly 10–12 centimeters (4–4 ½ inches) in length, 5–6 centimeters (2–2 ½ inches) wide, and 2 centimeters (¾ inch) in height. Alternatively, for finger-sized cakes, cut each block into smaller sticks.

11. Place the fruit cakes on the lined baking tray and bake in the oven for 20–22 minutes until golden and slightly burnt—that's one of the trademarks of this pizza, a little burnt on the outside but still moist inside! If you are making the smaller cakes, then 16–18 minutes baking time should be enough.

12. Remove from the oven, place on a cooling rack, and leave to cool for at least 20 minutes before serving.

13. The cakes will keep well in an airtight container for up to 2 weeks, or you can put a few into clear sachets to wrap and give as little presents.

SILVIA NACAMULLI is a London-based cook, born and raised in Rome, whose primary focus is Italian Jewish cuisine. She regularly contributes recipes for *The Jewish Chronicle*, and she is the author of *Jewish Flavours of Italy: A Family Cookbook* published by Green Bean Books. Follow her on her Instagram page @Silvia_Nacamulli and her blog cookingforthesoul.com.

SACHLAV: FRAGRANT AND CREAMY WARM MILK DRINK

Contributed by Mushka Hasklevich

PREP TIME: 2 minutes | **COOK TIME:** 5 minutes
TOTAL TIME: 7 minutes | **YIELD:** 4 servings

Sachlav is a creamy, comforting hot drink, thickened with cornstarch and scented with vanilla and rose. For me, memories of the shuk are bound up with smells. Walking through the small alleyways of the shuk on cold January mornings, enjoying rosy floral notes and the smell of sweet sachlav slowly brewing. I would always make a point to buy myself a cup of thick and comforting sachlav so that I could walk and shop in the shuk with a warm drink in my hand. Making it at home took me back immediately.

This recipe calls for almond milk and can be easily made with cow milk or other plant-based milks like soy, coconut, or oat.

Ingredients:

- 6 cups almond milk (or any milk of your choice)
- 5 tablespoons cornstarch
- 2 tablespoons sugar
- 1 tablespoon rose water
- 1 tablespoon salt
- 1 teaspoon vanilla extract
- 1 teaspoon cardamom

Toppings:
- Shaved coconut
- Cinnamon
- Cardamom
- Rose petals
- Nutmeg
- Pistachios

Tools:

- Measuring cups and spoons
- Microplane for grating whole spices
- Saucepan
- Whisk

Instructions:

1. In a saucepan, mix one cup of almond milk with cornstarch to create a slurry.
2. Add in the rest of the milk and ingredients and place over simmering heat.
3. Whisk for a few minutes until very thick and hot.
4. Add toppings and serve.

MUSHKA HASKELEVICH is a Middle Eastern Levantine chef. She spent eight years submersed in and exploring the food of the Mahane Yehuda market, the old traditions of Iraqi and Turkish cuisine, the seasonality of produce in Israel, and the heart and soul of the country. She now cooks seasonal Mediterranean food for clients and private dinner parties in NYC.

SEASONAL FRUIT COMPOTE

Contributed by Laurel Kratochvila

PREP TIME: 10 minutes, plus chilling time | **COOK TIME:** 45 minutes
TOTAL TIME: 55 minutes, plus chilling time | **YIELD:** 10–12 servings

Compote, a chilled fruit soup, is one of my favorite easy desserts. It's something light and sweet for after a big meal, plus it's a sophisticated dairy-free digestif. I like to make mine with a portion of whatever seasonal fruit is available—apples, plums, apricots, gooseberries, pitted cherries, and strawberries are all great additions.

Ingredients:

- 3 cups apples, peeled, cored, and cubed into 2-inch pieces
- 1–2 cups seasonal fruit of choice
- ¾ cup pitted prunes, whole
- ¾ cup dried apricots, cut in half
- ¾ cup yellow raisins
- ⅓ cup dark brown muscovado sugar
- 1 cup apple juice
- 1 cinnamon stick
- 4 cloves
- ½ lemon
- 3 tablespoons slivovitz or hazelnut liquor (optional)

Tools:

- Citrus juicer
- Cutting board
- Heat-proof bowl
- Large saucepan
- Measuring cups
- Sharp knife
- Spatula or wooden spoon

Instructions:

1. In a large saucepan, combine apples, seasonal fruit, prunes, apricots, raisins, sugar, apple juice, cinnamon, and cloves with 3 ½ cups of water (or enough to just cover all the fruit).
2. Bring the fruit to a boil, then cover, and reduce heat to a simmer and add liquor.
3. Simmer for 45 minutes, then remove from heat.
4. Squeeze in juice from half a lemon and stir.
5. Remove the cinnamon stick and the cloves, then pour the compote into a heat-proof bowl and cover.
6. Refrigerate until chilled.

NOTE: This will stay good in the fridge for about 10 days. Serve as is or enjoy for breakfast over yogurt or with muesli.

LAUREL KRATOCHVILA is a professional baker and the owner of Fine Bagels in Berlin, Germany. She lives with her husband, Roman, and her cat Meshka. She is also the author of *New European Baking*, an exploration of the new movement of artisan bakers across the continent. Laurel is passionate about Europe's returning Jewish bakery and food culture.

SPELT CARROT CAKE WITH COCONUT YOGURT FROSTING

Contributed by The Jewish Food Hero Kitchen

PREP TIME: 10 minutes | **COOK TIME:** 30 minutes
TOTAL TIME: 40 minutes | **YIELD:** 1 cake, serves 12

This vegan spelt carrot cake with coconut yogurt frosting is incredibly moist, with a tender crumb from the finely grated carrots and applesauce. It is delicately flavored with vanilla and ginger, though you can also add cinnamon, cloves, and nutmeg if you prefer a heavily spiced cake. It's delicious with or without frosting. This cake is wonderful to serve for Kiddush or Rosh Hashanah.

Ingredients:

- 1 cup + 3 tablespoons spelt flour
- 1 ½ teaspoons baking powder
- ½ teaspoon baking soda
- ¼ teaspoon ground ginger
- ¼ teaspoon salt
- ½ cup sugar (you can also use coconut sugar)
- 5 tablespoons applesauce
- 3 tablespoons coconut oil, melted
- ½ cup plant-based milk
- 2 teaspoons vanilla extract
- 1 cup finely grated carrots
- 1 cup thick coconut yogurt (or you can use Greek yogurt if not dairy-free)
- 1 tablespoon agave (or honey if not vegan)
- 1 tablespoon lemon juice

Tools:

- Baking pan, 11" x 7" or 13" x 9"
- Box grater
- Large mixing bowl
- Measuring cups and spoons
- Medium mixing bowl
- Parchment paper
- Small bowl
- Spatula
- Toothpick
- Vegetable peeler
- Whisk

Instructions:

1. Preheat the oven to 350°F and line an 11" x 7" baking pan with a piece of parchment paper. Alternatively, you can use a 13" x 9" baking pan, though the cake will be thinner.
2. In a large mixing bowl, whisk together the flour, baking powder, baking soda, ground ginger, and salt. Set aside.
3. In a medium mixing bowl, combine the sugar, applesauce, coconut oil, plant milk, and vanilla. Whisk until smooth.
4. Pour the wet ingredients into the dry and gently stir with a spatula until a smooth batter forms—don't overmix. Fold in the grated carrots.
5. Transfer the batter into the prepared pan and place in the oven to bake until the top is golden brown and a toothpick inserted into the center comes out clean, around 25–30 minutes.
6. Remove the cake from the oven and let it cool completely at room temperature.
7. In a small bowl, whisk together the coconut yogurt, agave, and lemon juice.
8. Spread the yogurt frosting on top of the cake and decorate as desired. Enjoy!

From The Jewish Food Hero Kitchen

SPICED DARK HONEY FRUIT CAKE

Contributed by Genie Milgrom

PREP TIME: 30 minutes | **COOK TIME:** 1 hour 15 minutes
TOTAL TIME: 1 hour 45 minutes
YIELD: 9" x 11" cake, 18–25 servings, depending on desired portion size

This recipe is from my book, *Recipes of My 15 Grandmothers.* All the rich fruits and honey make it perfect for Rosh Hashanah. Dark honey tends to have a stronger flavor than lighter colored varieties. The cake itself is rich but not overpowering, and it's beautiful with extra honey drizzled over it. This recipe is a keeper for the holidays for sure.

Ingredients:

- 2 cups flour
- 2 teaspoons allspice
- 2 teaspoons cinnamon
- ½ teaspoon nutmeg
- ½ teaspoon clove powder
- 1 cup turbinado sugar
- ½ cup margarine
- 3 large eggs, separated
- ¼ cup dark-colored thick honey
- 1 cup black raisins

- 1 ½ pounds of dried fruit, cut up small (apricots, figs, cherries, dates, and other fruits may be used. I did not use candied fruit as I felt it might be too sweet, so I used dried fruit instead)
- ¼ cup grape juice
- ½ teaspoon baking soda
- 1 tablespoon hot water
- Extra dark honey for serving, plus liqueur if desired

NOTE: Some varieties of dark or black honey include buckwheat, wildflower, thyme, dandelion, jarrah, chestnut, meadow, and manuka honey.

Tools:

- Electric beater
- Measuring cups and spoons
- Mixing bowls
- Parchment paper
- Rectangular glass mold, 9" x 11"
- Sieve
- Spatula
- Whisk

Instructions:

1. In a large bowl, mix and sift the flour, allspice, cinnamon, nutmeg, and clove powder three times.
2. In a separate bowl, beat the sugar and margarine together until creamy.
3. Separate the eggs.
4. Beat the egg yolks together with the honey.
5. Whip the egg whites with a whisk in a separate bowl.
6. Mix the egg yolk mixture together with the egg whites and the sugar and margarine mixture.
7. Add 1 ¾ cups flour slowly until well mixed.
8. Toss the raisins and cut-up fruits in the remaining ¼ cup flour and add to the mixture. Add the grape juice.
9. Dissolve the baking soda in hot water and add to the mixture.
10. Grease a large 9" x 11" rectangular glass mold and cover the bottom with greased parchment paper.
11. Put mixture into the mold and bake at 300°F for 1 hour 25 minutes. Check often for doneness.
12. Drizzle dark honey over the top with a little bit of liqueur if desired.

GENIE MILGROM is an award-winning writer with special expertise in ancestry and Crypto-Judaic Studies. She was born in Havana, Cuba, into a Roman Catholic family of Spanish ancestry. In an unparalleled work of genealogy, Genie fully documented her unbroken maternal lineage of 22 generations, back to 1405 and pre-Inquisition Spain and Portugal.

SUFGANIYOT CUPCAKES

Contributed by The Jewish Food Hero Kitchen

PREP TIME: 10 minutes | **COOK TIME:** 20 minutes
TOTAL TIME: 30 minutes | **YIELD:** 24 mini cupcakes (or 12 regular)

When the craving for doughnuts during Hanukkah wanes, make these delightful sufganiyot mini cupcakes. Capturing the essence of a baked, jam-filled doughnut, they are the perfect balance of moistness, a tender crumb, and just the right amount of sweetness. Serve them with a dollop of cottage cheese or Greek yogurt for extra protein.

Ingredients:

- 1 cup unsweetened soy milk
- 1 tablespoon apple cider vinegar
- ¼ cup coconut oil, melted
- ¼ cup unsweetened applesauce
- 1 teaspoon vanilla extract
- 1 ½ cups all-purpose flour
- 2 tablespoons cornstarch
- ½ cup sugar
- 1 teaspoon baking powder
- ½ teaspoon baking soda
- ¼ teaspoon salt
- 12 teaspoons sugar-free apricot jam
- ½ cup non-dairy Greek yogurt (for dairy version use cottage cheese or Greek yogurt)

Tools:

- Baking spray or paper liners
- Measuring cups and spoons
- Medium mixing bowl
- Mini muffin tin (or regular size)
- Spatula
- Whisk

Instructions:

---

1. Preheat the oven to 350 F and spray a mini muffin tin with non-stick baking spray. Alternatively, you can use paper liners.

2. Combine soy milk and vinegar in a medium bowl and allow to sit for 3 minutes.

3. Add the coconut oil, applesauce, and vanilla to the bowl with the soy milk and whisk until smooth.

4. Add in the flour, cornstarch, sugar, baking powder, baking soda, and salt. Whisk just until the dry ingredients are incorporated into the wet and a smooth batter forms—be careful not to overmix.

5. Divide the batter between 24 mini muffin holes and add ½ teaspoon of apricot jam on top of each. Place the muffin tin into the preheated oven and bake until the muffins are golden brown and puffed, around 15–20 minutes.

6. If desired, serve with a dollop of non-dairy yogurt (or cottage cheese or Greek yogurt).

From The Jewish Food Hero Kitchen

SUHALIKI: RUSSIAN BISCOTTI

Contributed by Toyoko Izaki

PREP TIME: 10 minutes | **COOK TIME:** 27 minutes
TOTAL TIME: 37 minutes | **YIELD:** 40–50 pieces

This Russian biscotti recipe arrived in Japan via the Russian Jews who founded the Jewish Community of Japan in 1953. They arrived primarily from Siberian cities like Harbin and Vladivostok, bringing their recipes with them. Although no descendants of the founding families remain in Japan, the community maintains fidelity to its origins by serving Suhaliki and other delicacies that have been consistently baked in the synagogue's kosher kitchen for decades.

This recipe was submitted by Rabbi Andrew Scheer to honor Toyoko Izaki.

Ingredients:

- 3 cups flour
- 2 teaspoons baking powder
- ½ teaspoon salt
- 1 cup sugar
- 1 cup oil
- 3 eggs
- 1 cup walnut halves, roughly chopped (not too small)
- 1 cup raisins

Tools:

- Large mixing bowl
- Measuring cups and spoons
- Medium mixing bowl
- Non-stick jelly roll baking sheet
- Parchment paper
- Sharp knife
- Spatula

Instructions:

1. Preheat the oven to 160°C.
2. Place parchment paper onto a non-stick jelly roll baking sheet.
3. In a medium bowl, mix flour, baking powder, and salt together.
4. In a separate large bowl, mix sugar, oil, and eggs.
5. Fold the dry ingredients into the wet ingredients and mix until well combined.
6. Add walnuts and raisins and mix until just combined.
7. Pour dough onto a parchment-lined baking sheet and spread out evenly—not too thin! Not too thick!
8. Bake for 20 minutes.
9. Remove from the oven and allow to cool for 10 minutes and then slice into thin rectangular slices.
10. Meanwhile, turn the oven temperature down to 140°C.
11. Place the slices back on the parchment-lined baking sheet and bake for another 7–8 minutes until golden brown.

TOYOKO IZAKI has been the baker at the Jewish Community of Japan since the early 1970s. A Ukrainian refugee who recently visited the synagogue described the aroma of Izaki-san's challah as reminiscent of her grandmother's home in Lviv.

TAHINI COOKIES

Contributed by Sivan Kobi

PREP TIME: 10 minutes | **COOK TIME:** 12–15 minutes
TOTAL TIME: 22–25 minutes | **YIELD:** 24 cookies

This is a Middle Eastern dream cookie with a shortbread-like texture that goes perfectly with any cup of hot tea or coffee. Made with simple pantry staple ingredients, these cookies will become a go-to favorite.

Ingredients:

- 2 cups plus 2 tablespoons all-purpose flour
- ¾ cup confectioners' sugar (powdered sugar)
- ¾ cup vegetable or canola oil
- ½ cup tahini (pure sesame paste)
- 1 tablespoon baking powder

For the topping:
- ½ cup slivered raw almonds

Tools:

- Baking sheet pan
- Measuring cups and spoons
- Mini scooper
- Parchment paper
- Stand mixer or bowl with mixing spoon

Instructions:

1. Preheat the oven to 350 F and line a baking sheet with parchment paper.
2. In no particular order, place all your ingredients, except the slivered almonds, in the mixer bowl. Mix for a couple minutes until it comes together to a nice batter. This can also be mixed by hand.
3. Using a mini scooper to ensure all your cookies are the same size, take scoops out and place them on the lined baking sheet.

4. Top each with a few slivered almonds right in the center. You want to make sure that you press the almonds into the cookie, otherwise they'll fall out.

5. Bake for about 12–15 minutes. They won't get too dark in color so make sure not to burn them. The bottom of the cookie will have a golden color.

6. Let them cool and enjoy.

SIVAN KOBI was born in Israel into a family of bakers. She grew up in Los Angeles where her parents owned three very successful bakeries and one deli. Her entire childhood was filled with memories from the bakery. She shares her passion for cooking and baking through community challah baking workshops and her Instagram page @sivanskitchen.

TANTE ROIZY'S HONEY CAKE

Contributed by Tiki Krakowski

PREP TIME: 25 minutes | **COOK TIME:** 1 hour | **TOTAL TIME:** 1 hour 25 minutes
YIELD: 10.75-inch bundt cake or 2 8-inch round cakes

My Great-Aunt Rose, or Tante Roizy, was a woman who knew her mind. She was strong-willed, worldly, competitive, especially when it came to Scrabble, and had a heart of gold. She earned her baking skills in her mother's Hungarian kitchen in Brooklyn and honed them in the South during a short stint in Memphis. Family legend is that she took this honey cake recipe from her own great-aunt, and then tinkered with it until it was to her liking.

Honey cake has a reputation of being dry and one-note, no matter how much spice you add. This one, by contrast, is moist and full of depth of flavor, despite the lack of ground spices. It has enchanted many honey-cake skeptics.

Ingredients:

- 6 eggs, separated
- 1 ½ cups sugar, divided
- 1 pound (16 ounces) honey
- 1 ⅓ cup coffee, cooled
- 1 teaspoon baking soda
- 2 teaspoons vinegar
- 3 cups flour
- 2 teaspoons baking powder
- Juice and zest of ½ orange

Tools:

- Citrus juicer
- Electric beater, handheld or standing
- Measuring cups and spoons
- Mixing bowls
- Non-stick angel food cake pan, bundt pan,
  or 2 non-stick 8-inch round cake pans

- Spatulas
- Whisk
- Zester

Instructions:

1. Preheat the oven to 325°F.
2. In a large bowl, mix 6 egg yolks, ½ cup sugar, honey, and coffee.

3. Put the baking soda in a little bowl and pour the vinegar over it. Let it bubble and foam. Add to egg yolk mixture.

4. In another large bowl, whisk together the flour, baking powder, and orange zest.

5. Starting and ending with the flour mixture, alternately add the flour and the orange juice to the egg-honey mixture. Set aside.

6. In a clean bowl, beat the egg whites until stiff peaks form. With the beaters running, slowly add 1 cup sugar. Beat until thick and marshmallow-like. Carefully fold the egg whites into the rest of the batter.

7. Pour the batter into the angel food cake pan, or evenly divide it into 2 ungreased 8-inch round pans. Tap the pans sharply on the countertop to eliminate air bubbles.

8. Bake for about an hour. The cakes are done when they spring back lightly to the touch.

9. Remove the cakes from the oven. Turn the cakes upside down and prop them up on evenly spaced cans to cool. When cool, turn right-side up.

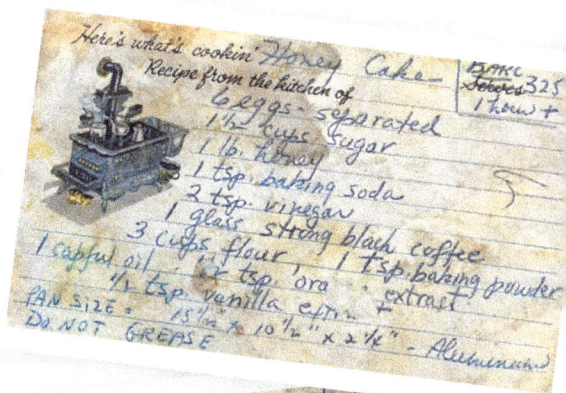

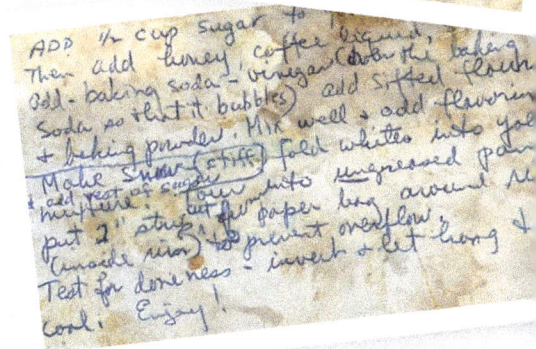

NOTE: If your cake pans have even the slightest bit of non-stick coating, DO NOT turn the cakes upside down. They will promptly fall out of their pans. Cool them right-side up on a wire rack.

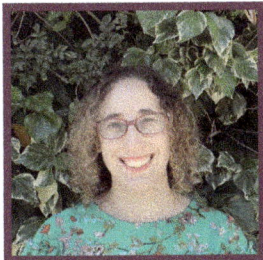

TIKI KRAKOWSKI is a translator, editor, and writer with a love of Jewish text. She has translated primary Jewish texts for *The New Koren Tanakh: The Magerman Edition*, and the *Posen Library of Jewish Culture and Civilization: Volumes 3 & 4*. Tiki enjoys geekery, baking, and feeding other people. She lives in Jerusalem with an excellent roommate, and her neurotic dog, River.

KARYN MOSKOW is a home cook who is passionate about keeping the Jewish festivals alive through her cooking. She loves to make traditional Jewish foods, continuing her 92-year-old mother's cooking traditions. Now her two daughters are following in her footsteps, which warms her heart.

TEIGLACH:
KNOTTED PASTRIES BOILED IN SYRUP

Contributed by Karyn Moskow

PREP TIME: 30 minutes, plus one hour resting time | **COOK TIME:** 35–45 minutes
TOTAL TIME: Approx. 2 hours | **YIELD:** 35–40 pastries

This is a recipe handed down from my Lithuanian grandparents who emigrated to South Africa in the 1940s. As a child I always remember the smell of the syrup every Yom Tov, when my mother, Ray Kibur, made them. It became a tradition to make these delicious biscuits for every Yom Tov and Simcha.

Teiglach are small, round pastries boiled in a ginger syrup. They are a traditional Ashkenazi Jewish treat.

Ingredients:

- 6 eggs, minus 1 white
- 2 tablespoons brandy
- 2 tablespoons sunflower oil
- 1 teaspoon caster (superfine) sugar
- 1 teaspoon ground ginger
- ½ teaspoon baking powder
- Finely grated zest of 1 large orange
- 3 cups cake flour, divided

For the syrup:
- 2 kilograms golden syrup
- 440 grams (2 cups) sugar
- 500 milliliters (2 cups) water
- 2 tablespoons ground ginger
- 500 milliliters (2 cups) boiling water

Tools:

- Benchtop
- Clean tea towel
- Kitchen scale
- Large baking tray
- Measuring cups and spoons
- Parchment paper
- Slotted spoon
- Stainless steel stock pot (preferably 20 liter / 20 quarts)
- Stand mixer with whisk and beater attachments
- Wooden spoon

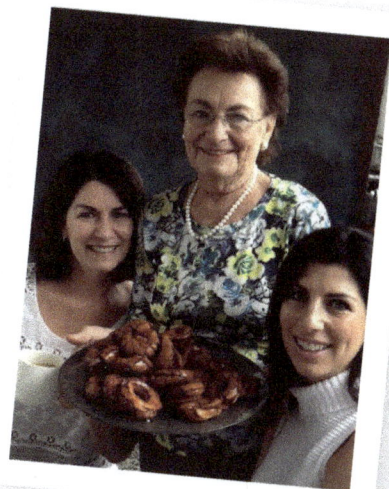

Instructions:

1. Line a large baking tray and sprinkle with flour.

2. In the bowl of the stand mixer, whisk the eggs for 5 minutes or until light and fluffy. Change to the beater attachment and add the brandy, oil, sugar, ginger, baking powder, and zest.

3. Add 2 cups of cake flour and mix gently. Slowly add the remaining 1 cup of cake flour a little at a time until the sticky dough is easy to handle.

4. Tip the dough onto a floured benchtop. Take a walnut-size piece of dough and with floured hands roll into a bagel shape. Another option is to roll them into walnut-size balls with a light touch and not squeezing the dough. Repeat until all the dough is shaped and placed on the prepared tray.

5. Place the tray outside (cover with a net if necessary) in the sun and allow to harden for approximately one hour. Turn halfway through. If there is no sun, place them in a low heat tepid oven to dry out for 30 minutes.

6. To cook the Teiglach, place the syrup, sugar, and water in a large pot. Tie a clean tea towel around the inside of the lid to prevent moisture from dripping into the pot whilst boiling.

7. Once the syrup is boiling, slip the teigels into the pot and cover with the lid. Give the pot a shake and wait to see the steam coming out of the top. Once this happens, reduce the heat to medium and boil gently for 20 minutes.

8. Remove the lid and very gently stir to coat all the teigels in syrup. Do this quickly, then replace the lid.

9. Ensure that the syrup continues to boil steadily, not too fast. Lift the lid and stir every 10 minutes or so until the teigels sound hollow and hard when tapped with a wooden spoon. This will take around 35–45 mins. Watch carefully towards the end so that the syrup doesn't burn: it needs to be dark and frothy, not burnt.

10. Add the ginger, stir again, and turn off the heat. Very carefully add the boiling water—beware, the syrup will splatter. Shield yourself with the lid of the pot.

11. Gently remove the teigels with a slotted spoon and place on baking paper on the benchtop. Store in an airtight container for up to 2 weeks and freeze for up to 2 months.

TORTOLICCHI: HARD DRY ALMOND COOKIES

Contributed by Vanessa Nostran

PREP TIME: 10–15 minutes | **COOK TIME:** 20 minutes
TOTAL TIME: 30–35 minutes | **YIELD:** 25 cookies, more depending on size

A traditional recipe of the Benè Romì, the Jewish Community in Rome, these hard, dry cookies feature honey and almonds. They are usually made for Purim, to celebrate a Bar/Bat Mitzvah, and for Mishmarot (wakes). A wake is usually on the night preceding a Brit Milah (circumcision), a wedding, the first night of Shavuot, Hoshanah Rabbah, and Rosh Hashanah. During the wake, it is customary to learn Talmud passages and recite hymns, Psalms, and kabbalistic passages. Participants receive a small sachet (chavod) containing tortolicchi and other sweets.

"Tortolicchio" (singular) derives from "tortore"—"stick" in Roman dialect, reflecting the biscuits' firmness and color. According to a Rav Isacco Lattes (1543), a married woman was given tortolicchio by her lover, associating the cookies with a somewhat aphrodisiac power.

Ingredients:

- 4 whole eggs
- 6 tablespoons sugar
- Pinch of salt
- 500 grams honey (just under 2 cups, or 17.64 ounces)
- 400 grams or 2 ½ cups almonds (natural, unbleached, whole or halved)
- Orange zest (from 1 orange)
- 1–2 pinches cinnamon powder (optional)
- Raisins (3 handfuls) (optional)
- 1 kilogram flour (6 cups + 3 tablespoons)
- 1 egg (for egg wash)

Tools:

- Kitchen scale
- Large mixing bowl
- Measuring cups and spoons
- Non-stick baking sheet
- Parchment paper
- Pastry brush
- Rolling pin
- Sharp knife
- Sieve (if you'd like)
- Spoon
- Whisk
- Zester

Instructions:

1. Preheat the oven to 180°C / 360°F.
2. In a large bowl, whisk the eggs with the sugar and salt.
3. Add the honey slowly, then the almonds and the orange zest. Combine using a spoon, making sure that all the ingredients are amalgamated evenly. You may wish to use warm honey (almost like a hot glue). Some like to add cinnamon and/or raisins.
4. Add the flour, ideally using a sieve for a more homogeneous dough. When the dough is firm, pour on a working surface (your table is just fine!). The dough should feel firm, sticky is ok, but not hard.
5. Using a rolling pin, spread the dough evenly: just over half an inch thick.
6. Prepare an oven tray: line it with baking paper and sprinkle some flour on the paper so the dough does not stick. Cut the dough into rectangular pieces (about 2.5 inches long, 1 inch wide) and place them on the tray.
7. Whisk 1 egg and use as an egg wash on top for a nice, brown final color.
8. Bake for about 20 minutes. When the cookies look brown, they are probably ready. You can check by taking a cookie out: if it snaps in half, it's ready! If it's still soft, leave the cookies in a little longer.

VANESSA NOSTRAN was born and raised in Italy, spent a decade in the UK, and is now based in Hong Kong where she is a high school math teacher. She loves authentic Italian food and likes to experiment with new ingredients. Except pineapple on pizza. When she's not marking schoolwork or on a school trip, Vanessa enjoys outdoor sports, hiking, and coasteering.

UPSIDE DOWN HONEY APPLE CAKE

Contributed by Rob Finkelstein

PREP TIME: 10 minutes, plus 20 minutes cooling time | **COOK TIME:** 55–60 minutes
TOTAL TIME: 90 minutes | **YIELD:** 8–12 servings

This moist, easy-to-make (no mixer necessary) cake is big on honey flavor without being overly sweet, and topped with delicious apples. The perfect dairy-free dessert for any occasion.

Honey cake is a traditional dessert for the Jewish holiday Rosh Hashanah, the Jewish new year. Growing up, I never saw honey cake and apple cake ideas combined. It was always a honey cake, and just apples dipped in honey. I loved the idea of an upside down apple cake, so I decided to combine the two for this perfect Rosh Hashanah dessert. This honey cake recipe is adapted from a recipe shared by my sister-in-law and her mother—both of whom are fabulous cooks!

Ingredients:

For the apple topping
(for the bottom of the pan):
- 55 grams (4 tablespoons) refined coconut oil, vegan butter, or margarine (or butter for a dairy version)
- 110 grams (½ cup) light brown sugar
- 1 teaspoon vanilla
- ¼ teaspoon salt
- 2 apples, cored and cut into at least ¼-inch wedges (see note below) (Granny Smith, Golden Delicious, Honeycrisp, Jonagold, Pink Lady)

For the honey cake batter:
- 240 grams (2 cups) all-purpose flour
- ½ teaspoon salt

- 2 teaspoons baking powder
- ½ teaspoon baking soda
- ¾ teaspoon cinnamon
- ¾ teaspoon allspice
- 2 large eggs
- 50 grams (¼ cup) sugar
- 396 grams (1 cup plus 2 ½ tablespoons) honey
- 110 grams (½ cup) neutral oil (vegetable, safflower, sunflower, canola, grapeseed)
- 156 grams (⅔ cup) strong coffee, at room temperature
- 1 teaspoon vanilla

Tools:

- Baking spray
- Cutting board
- Kitchen scale
- Measuring cups and spoons
- Metal spatula or knife
- Mixing bowls
- Mixing spoons
- Parchment paper

- Serving dish
- Sharp knife
- Spatula
- Springform pan, 9-inch
- Toothpick
- Vegetable peeler
- Whisk
- Wire rack

Instructions:

1. Preheat the oven to 350°F.
2. Spray a 9-inch springform pan with non-stick spray and line the bottom with a parchment paper round.
3. In a small bowl, whisk together the coconut oil, brown sugar, vanilla, and salt. Spread evenly into the prepared pan.
4. Place the sliced apples in a circular, decorative fashion over the brown sugar mixture, pressing them into it as you go.
5. In a separate small bowl, whisk together the flour, salt, baking powder, baking soda, cinnamon, and allspice. Set aside.
6. In a large mixing bowl, using the same whisk, whisk together the eggs and the sugar until fully combined. Whisk in the honey, oil, coffee, and vanilla.
7. Whisk the dry ingredients into the wet just until fully combined. Do not overmix.
8. Slowly pour the batter over the apples. (Pouring the batter too quickly may cause apples to float into the batter.) Bake for 55–60 minutes, until a toothpick pressed in the center comes out clean and the sides of the cake start to pull away from the pan.
9. Cool on a wire rack for 20 minutes.
10. Use a metal spatula or knife to release the cake from the sides of the pan. Release the clip from the side of the springform pan. Holding a serving dish over the cake, carefully invert the cake onto the serving dish. Remove the bottom of the pan and the parchment paper.
11. Allow to cool completely before slicing.

BAKING TIPS:

- Don't cut the apples too thin or they may float into the batter. Press the apples into the brown sugar mixture, and slowly pour the cake batter over the apples.
- For a dairy version, feel free to use butter in the brown sugar mixture.
- Be sure to use refined coconut oil: non-refined will bring a coconut flavor to the cake.
- Not all springform pans are created equally. Especially if your pan is at all misshapen, some of the liquid might ooze out from the bottom. When baking in a springform pan, I always place a baking sheet lined with foil on the rack below to catch any drippings. (I recommend doing this also for pies.)

- Feel free to add some sliced, toasted pecans on top of the apples just after inverting the cake onto the serving plate. As the brown sugar mixture cools to room temperature, the nuts will stay in place, adding additional decoration and texture to the cake.
- Store the cake covered well at room temperature. It tastes even better the second day. For an extended keep, store it in the refrigerator. It should last up to one week, but mine is always gone within a few days!

ROB FINKELSTEIN is a practicing lawyer who loves to bake (and eat) extremely delicious baked goods. He started baking when he was 12 and continued to bake as a stress reliever in law school, using a Barbie-sized oven in a tiny New York City studio apartment. He became a pastry chef and shares his recipes and baking tips on his blog, cinnamonshtick.com.

YOYOS: DONUT-SHAPED PASTRIES WITH PISTACHIO

Contributed by Marie-Claire Slama

PREP TIME: 15 minutes, plus 60 minutes resting time | **COOK TIME:** 15 minutes
TOTAL TIME: 90 minutes | **YIELD:** 25 servings

Yoyos are perfect for Hanukkah: they are festive donut-shaped Tunisian pastries sprinkled with crushed pistachios. The first Yoyos I tasted were deliciously homemade by Mamie Colette, the grandma of my husband. They are soaked with "Homemade Honey," an orange, lemon, and orange blossom infused syrup that can be prepared in advance and kept for months in a jar, as can the candied peels that are created in the process. Homemade Honey is delicious with many traditional Tunisian pastries.

Ingredients:

For the Yoyos:
- 3 eggs
- 3 tablespoons vegetable oil
- 3 tablespoons sugar
- ½ teaspoon vanilla essence
- 3 tablespoons orange blossom water
- Zest of 1 lemon
- 350 grams flour
- 22 grams baking powder
- 1 pinch of salt

For the Homemade Honey:
- 1 orange
- 1 lemon
- 1 kilogram sugar

- ½ teaspoon vanilla essence
- 3 tablespoons orange blossom water
- 3 tablespoons honey

To serve:
- Crushed pistachios

To deep fry the yoyo's:
- Vegetable oil, the amount of oil depends on the size of the pan

Tools:

- Citrus juicer
- Cling wrap or kitchen towel
- Cutting board
- Jars x 2
- Kitchen scale
- Large saucepan
- Measuring cups and spoons
- Mixing bowls
- Paper towels
- Plate
- Serving tray
- Sharp knife
- Small saucepan
- Spatula
- Stand mixer with a large mixing bowl
- Toothpick
- Zester

Instructions:

Make the Yoyos:

1. To the bowl of a stand mixer, add the eggs, oil, sugar, vanilla extract, orange blossom water, and lemon zest. Mix for 3 minutes until homogeneous.
2. In a separate bowl, mix the flour, baking powder, and salt together with a spatula, then add to the mixer bowl and continue mixing at low speed until the dough is smooth and slightly sticky.
3. Cover with cling wrap or kitchen towel and let stand at room temperature, away from drafts, for about an hour. While the dough is resting, prepare the "Homemade Honey."

Make the Homemade Honey:

4. Squeeze the orange and lemon into a small bowl and set the juice aside.
5. Cut the orange and lemon peel to 1cm thickness and add to a saucepan with enough water to cover 1cm above the peel.
6. Bring to a boil, then cook covered with a lid for 15 minutes on low heat.

7. Pour the sugar into the saucepan and stir until it dissolves.

8. Add the orange and lemon juice. Bring back to a boil, then add the vanilla and orange blossom water. Simmer on low heat for about 25 minutes without mixing.

9. Add the honey, stir, and continue simmering for an additional 15 minutes, or until the syrup is a little thick.

10. Take out the now candied peel and store in a small jar.

11. Pour the honey syrup into a jar and store until required.

Cook the Yoyos:

12. In a large saucepan over medium heat, pour enough vegetable oil to deep fry. A general guideline is to fill the pan with oil so that it's 2 to 3 inches deep.

13. Pour some more oil into a small bowl not far from the pan, to smear your hands during shaping.

14. With oiled hands, shape pieces of dough into balls a little larger than the size of a ping pong ball. Flatten slightly, then form a hole in the center by pressing the dough between the thumb and middle finger. Rotate the donut around the thumb and middle finger to smooth the shape.

15. Place the Yoyos into the hot frying oil, without overloading the pan. Fry for about 2 minutes until golden, then turn the Yoyos to brown the other side.

16. Drain the Yoyos on a plate lined with paper towels. With a toothpick, make a few small holes in the top side of each Yoyo. This will allow the Homemade Honey to penetrate the pastries.

17. Reheat the Homemade Honey syrup on low for a few minutes. When it has reached the desired consistency, dip the yoyos and turn them over so that they are well coated.

18. Drain above the pan to remove the excess honey syrup before placing them on a serving tray.

19. Sprinkle with crushed pistachios.

MARIE-CLAIRE SLAMA is passionate about innovation in health and life sciences, well-being, and sustainability. She has 20 years of global experience in digital innovation and business development for impactful change. She lives in Hong Kong with her husband and three children, and loves exploring new recipes with specific cultural heritage, personal significance, or special ingredients.

KOSHER FOR PASSOVER: DAIRY RECIPES

ALMENDRIKAS: CRANBERRY AND PRUNE HARD COOKIES DIPPED IN CHOCOLATE

Contributed by Nani Noam Vazana

PREP TIME: 40 minutes | **COOK TIME:** 15 minutes
TOTAL TIME: 55 minutes | **YIELD:** 36 pieces

Almendrikas are a sephardic hard, dry, sweet cookie. I remember my grandma would make them for the Mimouna, the traditional Maghrebi Jewish celebration dinner held the day after Passover, marking the return of eating Hametz. They always looked too good to be true, but after just one bite I felt I'd had too much—it was so sweet! I'd usually finish the evening with a stomachache.

Almendrikas are usually made with dates, and the recipe calls for actual hot boiling sugar to be poured into the mixture. In this updated recipe, I replace the dates with cranberries and prunes to make them more refreshing. I use stevia (or erythritol) to make them friendly both for diabetics and Keto diet practices. And they're even Kosher for Pesach! They were all gone the morning after the Seder.

Ingredients:

- 2 cups roasted and crushed almonds
- 1 cup chopped prunes
- 1 cup cranberries

- 2 eggs
- 100 grams melted butter (or non-dairy butter for pareve version)
- 2 tablespoons stevia (or erythritol) crystallized sweetener
- 2 tablespoons matzah meal (for non-passover version replace with 2 tablespoons corn flour)
- 1 tablespoon vanilla extract

For the topping:
- 400 grams 70% chocolate, melted

Tools:

- Baking sheet
- Cutting board
- Kitchen scale
- Measuring cups and spoons
- Mixing bowls
- Parchment paper
- Sharp knife
- Spatula
- Spoon

Instructions:

1. Preheat oven to 180°C.
2. Mix everything except the chocolate in a bowl with a spatula.
3. Divide the dough into three equal parts.
4. Flatten in 3 even rows on a baking sheet and bake for 20 minutes.
5. Remove from the oven when amber brown and cut immediately into bars.
6. Leave to cool for 30 minutes.
7. Once cooled, melt the chocolate.
8. Dip each almond bar until half-submerged in chocolate. Leave to set on a baking tray lined with parchment paper.
9. Enjoy! Pesah Alegre.

NANI NOAM VAZANA is the world's first Ladino songwriter. Her album *Ke Haber* (*What's New*) captures the spirit of the ancient, matriarchal culture and propels it into the 21st century with socially pertinent lyrics celebrating migration, gender, and female empowerment. Nani has won several awards and played at the Library of Congress and the Kennedy Center. She represented the Netherlands at the EU Music Festival in Vietnam.

CHOCOLATE SWISS ROLL

Contributed by Rabbi Jade Sank Ross

PREP TIME: 20 minutes | **COOK TIME:** 15 minutes
TOTAL TIME: 35 minutes, plus cooling time | **YIELD:** 10–12 servings

This is my family's traditional Passover dessert. It was adapted from *The Art of Fine Baking* by my grandmother, and then by my aunt who passed it on to me. The ingredients and preparation are light and simple, making a cake that is the perfect conclusion to a heavy meal and looks impressive on a holiday table.

NOTE: This recipe is best made the same day that you plan to serve it.

Ingredients:

- Cocoa for dusting
- 6 eggs, separated
- ¾ cup sugar
- 6 ounces semi-sweet chocolate, melted
- 2 tablespoons coffee
- 2 teaspoons vanilla
- 1 ½ cups heavy cream, whipped
- Confectioners' sugar for sweetening the cream to taste and for dusting

Tools:

- Cooking spray
- Electric mixer with whisk attachment
- Jelly roll baking sheet, 11" x 16"
- Large mixing bowls x 2
- Measuring cups and spoons
- Parchment paper
- Rubber spatula
- Serving platter, at least 12 inches long
- Sieve for dusting
- Small bowl for melting chocolate, plus microwave or bain-marie

Instructions:

1. Set the oven to 375°F.
2. Prepare the jelly roll pan by spraying it with cooking spray and lining it with a piece of parchment paper, so that the parchment paper sticks to the oil. Dust the top of the parchment paper with cocoa.
3. In a large mixing bowl, using an electric mixer, whisk the egg whites on high until they hold soft peaks. Then, lower the speed of the mixer and add sugar, one tablespoon at a time, continuing to whisk. Continue to whisk on high until the egg white and sugar mixture is glossy and holds stiff peaks. Set aside.
4. In a second large mixing bowl, use the electric mixer on high again to whisk the egg yolks until pale and fluffy. Continuing to whisk on a lower speed, slowly drizzle in the melted chocolate. Mix until completely incorporated. Continuing to whisk constantly, add the coffee and 1 teaspoon of vanilla. Mix until all ingredients are completely smooth.
5. Using a rubber spatula, fold ¼ of the egg whites into the chocolate and egg yolk mixture, taking care not to knock the air out. Continue with remaining egg whites until you have one uniform, light mixture.
6. Spread the batter evenly across the prepared jelly roll pan.

7. Bake for 10 minutes at 375°, then, without opening the oven door, lower the temperature to 350° and bake for another 5 minutes.

8. Remove the cake from the oven and cool completely in the pan. Alternatively, to make rolling a little easier and prevent cracks, when the cake is nearly cool but still slightly warm with the parchment paper still attached, loosely roll the cake and parchment starting at one short end, spiraling to the other. Then leave to cool.

9. Meanwhile, whip the cream with the remaining teaspoon of vanilla and the confectioner's sugar to taste (I use about 2 teaspoons).

10. When the cake is completely cool (if you did step 8, unroll the cake), spread the whipped cream evenly over the top side of the cake. Starting at one short end of the pan, carefully peel the parchment paper away from the cake while rolling the cake into a spiral. As you perform the final part of the roll to complete the spiral, roll the whole cake directly onto your serving platter, seam down. Dust with confectioner's sugar and enjoy.

RABBI JADE SANK ROSS grew up in Kinnelon, New Jersey. She graduated from Brandeis University and received her Rabbinic Ordination from Hebrew Union College—Jewish Institute of Religion. Currently, Jade serves as an Associate Rabbi at The Community Synagogue in Port Washington, NY. Jade, her husband, Rabbi Dan Ross, and their daughters love to cook and eat together and spend time with their dog, Rashi.

COTTAGE CHEESE BROWNIES

Contributed by The Jewish Food Hero Kitchen

PREP TIME: 10 minutes | **COOK TIME:** 25 minutes
TOTAL TIME: 35 minutes | **YIELD:** 9–12 brownies

I made these gluten-free cottage cheese brownies especially for Passover (and there's no matzo meal in these because too much matzo makes us constipated during Passover). They are very moist, fudgy, and packed with deep chocolate flavor in every bite. They are healthier than your average brownie recipe and high in protein from the cottage cheese, eggs, and almond flour. Make them a day ahead as the texture only gets better as the brownies sit out at room temperature. They will become your favorite brownie recipe!

Ingredients:

- ½ cup cottage cheese
- 2 large eggs
- 2 tablespoons coconut oil, melted
- 2 teaspoons vanilla extract
- 1 cup almond flour
- ½ cup unsweetened cocoa powder
- 1 cup coconut sugar (brown sugar also works, as does regular white sugar)
- ½ teaspoon baking soda
- ¼ teaspoon salt
- 2 ounces dark chocolate, roughly chopped

Tools:

- Blender or food processor
- Cutting board
- Large spoon
- Measuring cups and spoons
- Medium mixing bowl
- Parchment paper
- Sharp knife
- Square pan, 8" x 8"
- Whisk

Instructions:

---

1. Preheat the oven to 350°F and line a square pan with a piece of parchment paper.
2. Add the cottage cheese to a blender or a food processor and blend until smooth and creamy.
3. Transfer the cottage cheese into a medium mixing bowl and add in the eggs, coconut oil, and vanilla. Whisk until smooth.
4. Add in the almond flour, cocoa powder, sugar, baking soda, and salt. Gently fold the dry ingredients into the wet with a large spoon, just until a smooth mixture forms.
5. Chop the chocolate into smaller pieces.
6. Transfer the brownie batter to the prepared pan. Top the brownies with the chocolate pieces and place in the oven to bake for 22–25 minutes. The brownies will look a little wet when you pull them out, but they will set at room temperature.
7. Allow the brownies to cool before slicing. Serve sprinkled with flaky salt, if desired. Enjoy!

From The Jewish Food Hero Kitchen

DOUBLE CHOCOLATE TAHINI COOKIES

Contributed by Monica Glass

PREP TIME: 15 minutes | **COOK TIME:** 15–17 minutes
TOTAL TIME: 30 minutes | **YIELD:** 18 cookies

Slightly nutty and earthy flavored from tahini, ooey-gooey chocolatey, and tender with chewy centers and crisp edges, these cookies are a chocolate lover's dream come true. Oh, and they're gluten-free and wheat-free! I like to make a double batch ahead of time and freeze the dough for special gatherings—or so I can have a cookie whenever the craving hits.

Tahini is a paste made from ground hulled sesame seeds and is a staple in many cuisines. Beyond hummus, tahini is often used in savory recipes such as dressings, sauces, and dips, but it is versatile enough to be used in sweet recipes as well.

This recipe is kosher for Passover if you eat kitniyot and use kosher for Passover tahini.

Ingredients:

- 225 grams unsalted butter, room temperature
- 50 grams tahini
- 300 grams sugar
- 1 large egg, room temperature
- 3 grams vanilla extract
- 175 grams white rice flour
- 50 grams tapioca starch
- 55 grams cocoa powder, Dutch processed
- 3 grams baking powder
- 1.5 grams baking soda
- 6 grams salt
- 150 grams semi-sweet or dark chocolate chips

Tools:

- Baking sheet
- Handheld or stand mixer fitted with the paddle attachment
- Kitchen scale
- Measuring cups and spoons
- Non-stick baking mat or parchment paper
- Rubber spatula
- Small cookie scoop

Instructions:

1. Preheat the oven to 325°F.
2. In the bowl of a stand mixer fitted with the paddle attachment, cream together butter, tahini, and sugar until light and fluffy, about 3–5 minutes.
3. Add egg and vanilla, mixing to fully combine.
4. Mix in rice flour, tapioca starch, cocoa powder, baking powder, baking soda, and salt until well blended.
5. Fold in chocolate chips.
6. Using a cookie scoop, portion dough into rounds. Place on a baking sheet lined with parchment or a non-stick baking mat.
7. Bake in the preheated oven for 15–17 minutes until just nearly set. They should still be soft when touched and should appear under-baked.
8. Cool completely. Enjoy!

MONICA GLASS is an award-winning pastry chef, celebrated recipe creator, culinary consultant, and health and wellness advocate. Monica lives with Coeliac disease and is dedicated to empowering others with the confidence, creativity, and intuition to mindfully transform their relationship with food to create a nourished, joyful life. Monica and famed chef Ken Oringer are partners in Verveine Café & Bakery in Cambridge, Massachusetts, USA.

FLAN CUSTARD
WITH CREAM CHEESE AND BRANDY

Contributed by Roxana Levin

PREP TIME: 15 minutes | **COOK TIME:** 55 minutes
TOTAL TIME: 70 minutes | **YIELD:** 10 servings

This is my favorite recipe from my mom growing up in Argentina, even though it was not typical of her traditional Jewish cooking. I loved helping her make it and fighting with my brothers to lick the pan. It wasn't until I moved to the United States that I found out that "Filadelfia" is cream cheese!

Ingredients:

- 8 cups water
- 6 large free-range eggs
- 14-ounce can sweetened condensed milk
- 12-ounce can evaporated milk
- 8-ounce package cream cheese, softened
- ¼ cup brandy or similar liquor
- 1 tablespoon vanilla extract
- 2 ½ cups white sugar

Tools:

- Baking pan 4" x 10" (to make a bain-marie)
- Blender
- Bundt pan (flan mold)
- Butter knife
- Kettle or pot
- Measuring cups and spoons
- Serving platter
- Spatula
- Wire cooling rack

Instructions:

1. Preheat the oven to 350°F / 175°C.
2. Boil the water in a tea kettle or pot.
3. Blend all the ingredients except for the sugar and boiling water in a blender until it achieves a smooth consistency.
4. Pour the sugar into a bundt pan and heat on a stove top on medium heat. As the sugar melts and begins to turn brown, tilt carefully to coat the lower sides of the pan. Continue until all

the sugar is melted but not burned. Let it cool down.

5. Sit the bundt pan in the baking pan, then pour the boiling water into the baking pan.

6. Pour the blended mixture into the bundt pan.

7. Cook at 350°F for approximately 55 minutes.

8. Use a butter knife to check that the center of the flan is no longer liquid.

9. Place on a rack to cool to room temperature, then refrigerate for 3 hours.

10. Remove from the refrigerator 1 hour 30 minutes before serving.

11. Use a spatula to carefully help separate the flan from the edges of the bundt pan.

12. Place a serving platter on top of the bundt pan and invert the flan in one smooth, rapid motion so that the caramelized bottom ends up on top. Enjoy!

ROXANA LEVIN is originally from Argentina. She is a Spanish professor at St. Petersburg College in Tampa Bay, Florida. She shares her cheese flan with all her Spanish classes, friends, and family members. Roxana loves traveling, reading, exercising, and learning to cook with her husband. She lives in Palm Harbor, Florida, with her husband, two sons, and two sweet cats.

MOCHA GANACHE MACARON TART

Contributed by Sheri Silver

PREP TIME: 30 minutes | **COOK TIME:** 15 minutes
TOTAL TIME: 45 minutes | **YIELD:** 16 servings

This delicious tart is a perfect Passover dessert. The crust is a riff on an almond macaroon (my personal favorite of all macaroons) and the filling is a two-tone mocha ganache. The swirled effect is so easy, yet looks impressive, and the tart can be completed and kept in the fridge for up to a week in advance!

Ingredients:

For the crust:

- 1 cup whole almonds
- 1 cup granulated sugar
- 1 tablespoon Passover cake meal
- 1 teaspoon instant coffee
- 1 large egg white, at room temperature
- 2 teaspoons vanilla extract

For the chocolate ganache:

- 6 ounces bittersweet or semi-sweet chocolate, chopped
- 5 tablespoons heavy cream
- 2 tablespoons unsalted butter
- 1 tablespoon instant coffee

For the white chocolate ganache:

- 12 ounces white chocolate, chopped
- 5 tablespoons heavy cream
- 1 tablespoon instant coffee
- 2 tablespoons sour cream

For the garnish:

- 16 whole almonds

Tools:

- Cooking spray
- Fluted tart pan with removable bottom, 9-inch
- Foil
- Food processor
- Measuring cups and spoons
- Mixing bowls

- Piping bag with star tip
- Serving tray or platter
- Small knife
- Small saucepan
- Spatula
- Whisk

Instructions:

Make the crust:

1. Preheat the oven to 350°F. Line a 9" tart pan with a removable bottom with foil, pressing up the sides and into the grooves. Spray with a non-stick cooking spray.

2. Place the almonds, sugar, cake meal, and instant coffee in a food processor and process until finely ground. Add the egg white and vanilla and process just until a ball forms on the side of the bowl. Transfer to your prepared pan and press into an even layer on the bottom of the pan (damp fingers will facilitate this).

3. Bake until the crust looks dry and feels firm, about 15 minutes. Let cool completely in the pan.

Make the chocolate ganache:

1. Place the chopped chocolate in a bowl.

2. Heat the heavy cream, butter, and instant coffee in a small saucepan over low heat, stirring constantly. Pour over the chocolate and whisk until smooth and glossy. Set aside and clean out the saucepan.

Make the white chocolate ganache:

1. Place the chopped white chocolate in a bowl.

2. Heat the heavy cream and instant coffee, stirring constantly, until hot. Pour over the white chocolate and whisk until smooth. Add the sour cream and whisk again. Pour ½ cup of the ganache into a small bowl and place in the fridge (this will be used to pipe on the finished tart).

Assemble the tart:

1. Dollop the chocolate ganache onto the crust, leaving gaps. Dollop the white chocolate ganache in between, then use a small knife to swirl together. Freeze for about an hour, until firm. Check the reserved white chocolate ganache; it should be firm enough to pipe (you can freeze it for a few minutes if it is still soft).

2. Use the foil to lift the tart from the pan. Turn it on its side and carefully peel off the foil. Place the tart on your serving tray or platter.

3. Transfer the reserved white chocolate ganache to a piping bag fitted with a star tip. Pipe 16 rosettes around the edge of the tart and top each rosette with an almond.

4. Refrigerate until firm, then cover and keep in the fridge for up to one week.

> **NOTES:** Chocolate chips may be substituted for the bittersweet and white chocolates. All-purpose flour, gluten-free flour, or almond flour may be substituted for the cake meal.

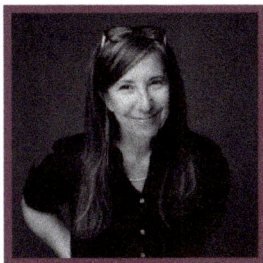

SHERI SILVER is a lifelong New Yorker and has been writing her blog sherisilver.com for over 12 years. When not in the kitchen preparing, styling, and shooting food, she can be found wandering around her beloved city with her husband and/or 3 kids (usually in search of food).

PAVLOVA WITH DESERT LIME CURD
AND MACADAMIA PRALINE

Contributed by Natalie Levy

PREP TIME: 1 hour | **COOK TIME:** 1 hour
TOTAL TIME: 2 hours | **YIELD:** 12–16 slices

Whether you believe Pavlova originated in Australia or New Zealand, this one definitely represents Australia with its prominent use of native desert lime and macadamia. With its crisp and sugary meringue, smooth and tangy curd, and crunchy praline, this dessert offers a tantalizing experience for your taste buds. It can be made dairy or pareve by substituting butter with margarine. It is a family favorite during Pesach. Furthermore, it can be easily customized with different citrus fruits and nuts. An alternative variation featuring orange curd and pistachio praline also creates a delightful flavor combination.

Ingredients:

For the pavlova:

- Vinegar to wipe bowl down
- 16 large egg whites at room temperature
- Pinch of salt
- 1 kilogram caster sugar
- 4 tablespoons cornstarch
- Squeeze of lemon

Desert lime curd:

- ½ cup lime zest (from approximately 7 limes)
- 500 grams granulated sugar
- 8 large egg yolks
- 4 large eggs
- 240 milliliters freshly squeezed lime juice
- 170 grams cold unsalted butter, cubed

Macadamia praline:

- ½ cup unsalted macadamia nuts, coarsely chopped
- 1 cup caster sugar

Tools:

- Baking tray
- Handheld beater or stand mixer with whisk attachment
- Kitchen scales
- Large mixing bowl
- Measuring cups and spoons
- Medium glass bowl
- Medium mixing bowl
- Parchment paper
- Piping bag and tips
- Pot (to create double boiler)
- Sieve
- Small non-stick frying pan
- Spatula or spoon for spreading curd
- Whisk
- Zester

Instructions:

For the pavlova:

1. Set the oven to 120°C / 350°F.
2. Wipe down the bowl with vinegar.
3. Beat egg whites, add salt, and slowly add sugar. Beat until glossy. Pinch a bit of the mixture between your fingers and rub together to ensure the mixture is not gritty.
4. Add cornstarch and squeeze of lemon.
5. On a baking tray lined with paper, spread mixture into 8-inch rounds.
6. Pipe mini meringues for decoration.
7. Bake for approximately 40 minutes, then leave in the oven to cool.

Make the Desert Lime Curd:

8. Rub zest and sugar together until fragrant.
9. Set up a pot of water to create a double boiler.
10. Whisk yolks and eggs in a medium glass bowl.
11. Add zest and sugar, continuing to whisk.
12. Add lime juice.
13. Add cold butter and whisk in the glass bowl over the double boiler until thickened to the consistency of sour cream.
14. Remove from heat, strain to remove any lumps, and cool.

Make the Macadamia Praline:

15. Preheat the oven to 180°C fan-forced.

16. Line a baking tray with non-stick baking paper. Spread the macadamias over the tray. Roast in the oven for 5 minutes, or until lightly toasted.

17. Place the sugar in a small non-stick frying pan over a low heat. Tilt the pan back and forth until sugar dissolves and turns to toffee (do not stir). Pour the hot toffee over the warm macadamia nuts. Set aside to cool.

18. Break into shards.

Assemble the pavlova:

19. Spread the curd on each layer of the meringue and top with macadamia praline shards.

NOTES: Desert limes can be difficult to find even within Australia. You can use regular limes as an alternative.

NATALIE LEVY is a baking enthusiast and business owner. Natalie's baking draws on her English, Russian, and Jewish heritage, bringing a unique fusion of flavors and techniques to her creations. Natalie's innovative approach led her to be a contestant on *The Great Australian Bake Off* in 2023 and to launch and run a thriving baking company. Find her on Instagram @sweet_as_funk.

PERSIAN LOVE CAKE

Contributed by Joanna Nissim

PREP TIME: 15 minutes │ **COOK TIME:** 35 minutes
TOTAL TIME: 50 minutes │ **YIELD:** 10 generous portions

I was recently asked to submit a Pesach recipe to a local newspaper. I chose the beautiful Persian Love Cake which I have long adored. I spent time making and photographing it and as always served it to my family who are my tasters. Sadly, a week after this, my chief taster, my daddy, unexpectedly passed away. And so, the Persian Love Cake is dedicated to him, and I will always think of him when I make it. This recipe can easily be made pareve.

Ingredients:

- 150 grams butter (or non-dairy butter), cubed
- 120 grams sugar
- 3 eggs
- 200 grams ground almonds
- 100 grams ground pistachio
- 1 tablespoon rose water
- 1 teaspoon ground cardamom
- 1 teaspoon baking powder
- Juice and zest of 1 large orange

For the syrup to drizzle on top:
- ¼ cup honey
- A generous splash of rose water

Tools:

- Baking spray or parchment paper
- Electric beaters
- Measuring cups and spoons
- Mixing bowl
- Silicone cake tin
- Skewer
- Small saucepan to make the syrup
- Spatula

Instructions:

1. Preheat the oven to 180°C.
2. Beat the cubed butter and sugar together until light and creamy.
3. Add in the 3 eggs and mix well.
4. Mix in the remaining ingredients: ground almonds, pistachio, rose water, cardamom, baking powder, and zest and juice of the orange.
5. Spray a silicone cake tin or line with parchment and pour the mixture in.
6. Bake for approximately 35 minutes until a skewer comes out clean.
7. Once cooked, take the cake out of the oven, and leave to cool in the tin.
8. Whilst it is cooling, make the drizzle by warming the honey and rose water.
9. Once the cake has cooled and is turned out onto the serving dish, drizzle the syrup all over.
10. Decorate with edible rose petals and crushed pistachio.

JOANNA NISSIM is a wife, mother of two, food writer, and passionate cook living in London. She hosts cooking demonstrations and private classes, and every Shabbat she cooks and sells Sephardi shabbat dishes. To preserve her family's Sephardi recipes, Joanna wrote a cookbook which she hopes to publish. Her recipes and handy tips can be found on her Instagram page @Joanna_nissim.

POMEGRANATE MOLASSES
CHOCOLATE FUDGE

Contributed by Gaby Ross

PREP TIME: 10 minutes | **SETTING TIME:** 2 hours
TOTAL TIME: 2 hours and 10 minutes | **YIELD:** 16 squares

I first made this pomegranate fudge when I was in college, sharing an apartment with my twin brother, and about to host my first Rosh Hashanah. Our parents were driving three hours to join us, and I quickly whipped up this fudge for our holiday dessert. My family has always expressed our love and Jewishness through food, and as Sephardim, flavors like rose, orange blossom, and pomegranate were staples I grew up with. This dessert easily became a go-to to bring to potlucks and events. It's easy to make these vegan too! This recipe is perfect for Rosh Hashanah but also kosher-for-Passover too.

Ingredients:

- 24 ounces (680 grams) semi-sweet chocolate chips
- 14-ounce can (400 grams) of sweetened condensed milk (substitute condensed coconut milk for vegan or pareve)
- ¼ cup pomegranate molasses
- Seeds from one whole pomegranate

Tools:

- Dish, 9" x 9"
- Kitchen scale
- Measuring cups and spoons
- Microwave
- Microwave-safe bowl
- Parchment paper
- Sharp knife
- Spatula

Instructions:

___

1. In a microwave-safe bowl, pour the can of condensed milk over the chocolate chips.
2. Microwave the chocolate in 30 second increments, stirring in between until the mixture is completely melted. This should take about 90 seconds.
3. Once melted, add the pomegranate molasses and mix until it's smooth.
4. It will be very thick, but pour it into the parchment-lined pan and use the spatula to flatten it into an even layer.
5. Add the pomegranate seeds to the top of the fudge and pat gently so that they stick.
6. Put the fudge in the fridge to set for at least two hours.
7. Cut into squares to serve.

GABY ROSS is a special education teacher and amateur cake-decorator, who loves creating desserts with unusual flavor combinations. When she is not in the kitchen, she is making jewelry, crafting, and playing board games. She lives in Dallas, Texas, with her family and her dog, Latke.

KOSHER FOR PASSOVER: PAREVE RECIPES

BOCCA DI DAMA: NUTTY VANILLA SPONGE CAKE

Contributed by Azelma Moscati

PREP TIME: 10 minutes | **COOK TIME:** 30 minutes
TOTAL TIME: 40 minutes | **YIELD:** 14 servings

I first discovered this soft, almondy sponge cake called Bocca di Dama when my brother and I experienced Passover with a Libyan family. I loved it so much that I searched for the recipe and found it in one of my favorite cooking books: *La cucina ebraica tripolina* by Linda Guetta Hassan.

I share my version here, with adaptations. I combine almond and hazelnut flour for a nuttier taste. I use vanilla, but you can also use lemon zest or almond extract. Dark brown sugar brings a delicious, caramelized taste to the cake.

Ingredients:

- 4 eggs, separated
- 200 grams brown sugar
- 200 grams almond flour
- 100 grams hazelnut flour
- 2 tablespoons fine matzo flour
- 1 teaspoon vanilla extract (or lemon zest or almond extract)
- 2 tablespoons slivered almonds

Tools:

- Cake pan
- Hand mixer or whisk
- Kitchen scale
- Large mixing bowl
- Measuring cups and spoons
- Parchment paper
- Small mixing bowl
- Spatula
- Toothpick

Instructions:

1. Preheat the oven to 350°F / 175°C and line a cake pan with parchment paper.
2. In a small mixing bowl, whisk the egg whites until stiff. Set aside.
3. In a large mixing bowl, whisk together sugar and egg yolks. Once smooth and fluffy add the almond flour, hazelnut flour, matzo flour, vanilla extract (or lemon zest or almond extract).
4. Once all mixed, gently fold in the egg white, mixing from top to bottom with a spatula in order to keep them properly whipped.
5. Spread the mixture evenly in the prepared cake pan and smooth out with the spatula.
6. Add slivered almonds on top.
7. Bake for 20–30 minutes, or until a toothpick inserted into the center comes out clean, and allow to cool for 15 minutes.
8. Cut into 14 slices and enjoy!

AZELMA MOSCATI is an Italian mother of four who loved baking from an early age. After completing a professional patisserie course, she finished a BA in journalism. Currently she works as an online marketing consultant from Gibraltar. She's always on the web searching for new and better recipes to serve at home to family and friends.

CHOCOLATE TRUFFLES

Contributed by Maya Maizlech

PREP TIME: 10 minutes, plus 2–3 hours chilling time | **COOK TIME:** 0 minutes
TOTAL TIME: 2 hours 10 minutes | **YIELD:** 10 balls

These chocolate truffles are a melt-in-your-mouth chocolate experience in a ball. Best of all, they're gluten-free, dairy-free, refined-sugar–free, and vegan. Sure, they're Passover-friendly, but I make these all year round!

Ingredients:

For the truffles:
- 1 cup (120 grams) almond flour
- ¼ cup (55 grams) cacao powder
- 3 tablespoons maple syrup
- 2 tablespoons coconut oil
- 1 teaspoon vanilla
- ¼ teaspoon salt
- ¼ cup (50 grams) dark chocolate chips

For the chocolate coating (optional):
- 1 cup (175 grams) dark chocolate
- 1 tablespoon coconut oil

Tools:

- Baking tray
- Fork
- Medium mixing bowl
- Parchment paper
- Saucepan (for bain-marie) or microwavable glass bowl (optional)
- Spatula or wooden spoon

Instructions:

1. Mix together all the ingredients, except the chocolate chips, in a medium mixing bowl with a spatula or wooden spoon until well combined.

2. Fold in the chocolate chips, roll into balls, and place on baking tray lined with parchment paper.

3. Freeze for at least 1 hour (or overnight).

4. When ready to shape and coat the truffles, melt the dark chocolate and coconut oil together until smooth (if using). You can do this with a bain-marie or short blasts in a microwave, stirring in between.

5. Dip each truffle in the melted chocolate with a fork and place back onto parchment.

6. Place in the fridge for 1–2 hours to harden before serving. If you are in a hurry, place in the freezer for 30 minutes.

MAYA MAIZLECH is an Integrative Nutrition Health Coach and wellness educator, who believes there is more to health than running marathons and banning carbs. Holistic wellness involves nourishment from lifestyle as much as from food. Maya advocates for embracing a balanced diet full of whole foods, developing a positive mindset, and practicing good habits and wholesome routines.

COCONUT CREAM FRUIT SORBET

Contributed by Aliza Grubin

PREP TIME: 15 minutes, plus 6 hours chilling time | **COOK TIME:** 0 minutes
TOTAL TIME: 6 hours 15 minutes | **YIELD:** 6–7 servings

As a chef I always need to come up with simple delicious recipes that are good for everyone. In 2023, I decided to eat more whole food plant-based foods so I wanted a new and refreshing dessert. I came up with this sorbet and was so happy with it that I decided to make it for the following Shabbat. Everyone went crazy over it—even the kids! I can't wait to make it for Passover because it's a great recipe to share with everyone. Enjoy!

Ingredients:

- 2 ½ cups frozen mango
- 1 cup frozen strawberries
- 1 cup coconut cream
- 2 tablespoons maple syrup
- Zest of 1 small lemon
- Pinch of salt

Tools:

- Food processor or blender
- Freezer safe container
- Measuring cups and spoons
- Spatula

1. Place all the ingredients into a food processor or blender, and blend until smooth and creamy.
2. Place it into a container and freeze for about 6 hours and serve.
3. Tip: For a creamier sorbet, after 6 hours in the freezer, let it soften and then blend it a second time and freeze for an additional 4 hours.

ALIZA GRUBIN is an accomplished personal chef and inventive recipe developer in Israel who focuses on dietary restrictions like gluten-free, refined sugar-free, and vegan options. Her culinary creativity extends to fun and exciting meals, making every bite a unique experience. For a taste of her diverse and flavorful creations, follow Aliza on Instagram at @Aliza_personal_chef.

COQUITOS:
COCONUT MACAROONS

Contributed by Deborah Sandler

PREP TIME: 10 minutes | **COOK TIME:** 10 minutes
TOTAL TIME: 20 minutes | **YIELD:** 24 coquitos

"Coquitos," also known as "cocadas," are traditional Argentine sweets that I serve for Passover. They have their origin in the Creole culture and the tradition of using coconut in cooking. It's believed that the recipe was influenced by cocadas prepared in other Latin American countries. Their popularity has endured over the years, making them a distinctive sweet of Argentine culture.

The basic recipe consists of mixing grated coconut and sugar, ingredients that were accessible and abundant in the region. They are shaped into pyramids and baked until they turn golden brown.

Ingredients:

- 1 cup sugar
- 2 ¼–2 ½ cups shredded coconut
- 2 eggs
- 1 ½ cups (12 ounces) kosher for Passover pareve chocolate chips (optional)

Tools:

- Baking tray
- Large mixing bowl
- Measuring cups and spoons
- Parchment paper
- Silicone baking mat (optional)
- Small mixing bowl
- Whisk

Instructions:

1. Preheat the oven to 180°C / 356°F.
2. Place the sugar and 2 ¼ cups of coconut in a medium bowl.
3. Beat the eggs in a small bowl with a whisk and add them to the mixture. If needed, add more coconut.
4. Knead with your hands until you get a homogeneous paste.
5. Form small balls and shape them into cones. Place them on a baking tray lined with parchment paper.
6. Bake for 10 minutes.
7. If adding chocolate: once coquitos have cooled, melt chocolate chips according to package directions.
8. Dip ½ of each coquitos into melted chocolate, then transfer to a baking sheet that is covered with a silicone baking mat or parchment paper. Allow chocolate to set completely, typically taking 1–2 hours.

DEBORAH SANDLER is originally from Argentina, where all four of her grandparents immigrated from Poland. Deborah moved to the United States and graduated from fashion school before finding her path in Torah observance during her college years. Through her business, Joy of Cholov, Deborah shares the flavors of her heritage and her passion for fusing traditions, family history, and crafting experiences.

LEMON SQUARES

Contributed by Rachel Berger

PREP TIME: 15 minutes | **COOK TIME:** 50 minutes
TOTAL TIME: 1 hour 5 minutes plus chilling time | **YIELD:** 24 squares

This recipe is a Passover adaptation of my popular lemon squares. It is a nice change from your typical sponge cake or brownie. I love the tangy and refreshing lemon flavor, which is an unexpected dessert flavor on Passover. This recipe can be made in advance and freezes well.

Ingredients:

For the bottom crust:
- 1 cup matzah cake meal
- 1 cup potato starch
- ½ cup powdered sugar
- 1 cup non-dairy butter (use butter for a dairy version)

For the lemon filling:
- 4 large eggs, at room temperature
- 2 cups granulated sugar
- ⅓ cup fresh lemon juice
- 1 teaspoon lemon zest
- ½ teaspoon baking powder

For serving:
- Powdered sugar

Tools:

- Baking pan, 9" x 13"
- Measuring cups and spoons
- Sharp knife
- Small bowl
- Spatula
- Stand mixer with paddle attachment

Instructions:

1. Preheat the oven to 350°F.

2. Prepare the crust: Combine the matzah cake meal, potato starch, and powdered sugar in the bowl of a stand mixer fitted with the paddle attachment. With the mixer on low, slowly add the melted butter or margarine, until the mixture comes together.

3. Pat the mixture evenly into the baking pan, and about an inch up the sides.

4. Place the pan in the middle rack of the oven and bake for 25 minutes, or until golden around the edges.

5. While the crust is baking, prepare the filling: break up the eggs in the bowl of a stand mixer. Add the sugar, lemon juice, zest, and baking powder. Combine well, but don't mix too hard—you don't want it to get frothy.

6. Pour the filling into the crust, while the crust is hot. (It's best to time it so you prepare the filling to coincide with the crust baking.)

7. Continue to bake for an additional 25 minutes or until set in the middle. If the filling starts to brown too much, cover loosely with foil.

8. Cool the lemon squares in the pan, then cover with plastic wrap or aluminum foil and refrigerate for at least 2 hours. You can refrigerate overnight to enhance the flavor.

9. Before serving, dust with powdered sugar, and cut into 24 squares.

RACHEL BERGER is a recipe developer, food photographer, and food blogger at thekosherdinnerlady.com. She hosts cooking classes and demonstrations, runs a summer cooking camp for kids, and sells kosher custom celebration cakes for any occasion.

MARZIPAN

Contributed by Sylvia Fallas

PREP TIME: 20 minutes, plus 3 hours chilling time | **COOK TIME:** 0 minutes
TOTAL TIME: 3 hours 20 minutes | **YIELD:** 2 12-inch logs or 48 golf ball–size candies

Marzipan is a "special occasion" confection that is sliced or molded. It's often served at Syrian life cycle events and displayed on small mirrors or crystal dishes. Small pieces are arranged alongside other sweets like chocolate-dipped candied citrus and tiny almond cookies. While marzipan is an old-fashioned candy, it's still popular among the younger generations. Traditional recipes are lengthy and require many steps to prepare the almonds. I take a shortcut and use almond flour, which is made from blanched almonds with their skins removed.

Ingredients:

- 4 cups almond flour
- 2 ¼ cups powdered sugar
- 1 teaspoon vanilla extract
- Scant ½ cup water
- 1 cup dark chocolate chips
- 1 teaspoon coconut oil
- Crushed nuts (optional)
- Sprinkles (optional)

Tools:

- Baking tray
- Cling wrap (optional)
- Food processor (not a blender)
- Measuring cups and spoons
- Microwave-safe bowl
- Rubber spatulas x 2
- Waxed paper

Instructions:

1. Add the almond flour and powdered sugar to a food processor fitted with the standard curved blade. Pulse 10–15 times, or until the mixture is incorporated and sandy in texture.
2. Add the vanilla through the feed tube. Turn the machine on low and slowly drizzle in half of the water. The mixture will start to clump into a ball with the texture of cookie dough.

Stop the machine and use a rubber spatula to scrape down the mixture. Drizzle in more water as needed. Depending on your brand of almond flour and your food processor, you may need less than the ½ cup water.

3. Once the mixture forms a ball, remove the blade and begin to shape the marzipan.

4. Shape the marzipan:

    SLICED MARZIPAN: Split the mixture in half. Cut a piece of waxed paper approximately 8" x 11". Using wet hands, shape the dough into a log and place in the center of the waxed paper. Use the waxed paper to gently shape into a log, twisting the ends to secure. Repeat with the other half of the marzipan mixture. Wrap it up in cling wrap and refrigerate for at least one hour. It will firm up slightly in the refrigerator. Then slice.

    MOLDED MARZIPAN: Line a baking tray with waxed paper. With wet hands, pinch walnut-sized balls of marzipan. Gently roll into small balls and place on waxed paper. Freeze your marzipan until solid, about three hours.

5. To decorate the marzipan, prepare your chocolate for dipping. Combine chocolate chips and coconut oil in a microwave-safe bowl. Microwave at 30 second intervals, until chocolate is melted and glossy. Stir with a rubber spatula.

6. Carefully dip pieces or balls of marzipan into chocolate mixture, leaving some marzipan plain. The goal is a two-toned effect. Optional: dip into crushed nuts or sprinkles before chocolate hardens.

7. Refrigerate or freeze until ready to serve. Note: marzipan can be stored in the freezer plain and dipped before serving.

SYLVIA FALLAS is a Brooklyn-based food blogger, cooking instructor, and private chef. She teaches Jewish cultural cooking to students of all ages, weaving Jewish history into her lessons and showing how Jewish cuisine truly is a melting pot. Although she has a BA in Health and Nutrition Sciences, she's not afraid of butter! Follow her cooking adventures on Instagram @sylviafallas.

MINI NUT AND SEED BARS

Contributed by The Jewish Food Hero Kitchen

PREP TIME: 10 minutes | **COOK TIME:** 30 minutes
TOTAL TIME: 40 minutes | **YIELD:** 12–16 bars

These mini nut and seed bars are perfectly sweet and salty, with a delicious crunch. They are also packed with plant protein and fiber from the nuts and seeds. We've used a combination of almonds, walnuts, and pumpkin seeds to keep them kosher for Passover, though you can use a mix of any nuts and seeds that you like. Keep them in a sealed container at room temperature so the bars stay as crunchy as possible.

Ingredients:

- ¾ cup raw almonds
- ½ cup walnuts
- ¾ cup raw pumpkin seeds
- 2–3 tablespoons honey (or maple syrup)
- 2 teaspoons melted coconut oil
- 2 teaspoons vanilla extract
- ¼ teaspoon salt

Tools:

- Chopping board
- Measuring cups and spoons
- Medium mixing bowl
- Parchment paper
- Sharp knife
- Spatula or wooden spoon
- Square pan, 8" x 8"

Instructions:

1. Preheat the oven to 325°F and line a square pan with a piece of parchment paper.

2. Roughly chop half of the almonds and all of the walnuts.

3. Add the chopped nuts, the whole almonds, and the pumpkin seeds to a medium bowl and stir briefly with a spatula or wooden spoon.

4. Add in the honey, coconut oil, vanilla, and salt. Mix well until all the nuts and seeds are lightly coated in the oil and honey.

5. Transfer the nut and seed mixture into the prepared pan and place in the oven to bake until lightly golden on top, around 25–30 minutes.

6. Allow to cool for at least 30 minutes—this will help the nuts really crisp up—then slice into bars and enjoy!

From The Jewish Food Hero Kitchen

MIXED BERRY COBBLER

Contributed by The Jewish Food Hero Kitchen

PREP TIME: 10 minutes | **COOK TIME:** 30 minutes
TOTAL TIME: 40 minutes | **YIELD:** 4–6 servings

Finally a fruit Passover dessert recipe! This mixed berry cobbler is made with frozen berries because in my opinion it's criminal to cook fresh berries! Ripe berries should be eaten fresh and savored: frozen berries are ideal for smoothies and baked desserts, where form and sweetness don't matter. This berry cobbler comes together in less than 10 minutes and can easily be doubled to serve a crowd. It is vegan and gluten-free, yet tastes rich and decadent. Try adapting it with apples and cinnamon, pear and plums, or even ripe persimmons.

Ingredients:

- 300–350 grams frozen mixed berries
- 1 tablespoon tapioca flour
- ¼ cup + 2 tablespoons sugar
- 1 teaspoon lemon juice
- 1 cup almond flour
- ½ cup potato starch
- 2 tablespoons coconut flour
- 1 teaspoon baking powder
- ¼ teaspoon salt
- ¼ cup coconut oil, melted
- ⅓ cup unsweetened soy milk
- 1 teaspoon vanilla extract

For serving:
- Powdered sugar
- Plant-based yogurt
- Plant-based ice cream

Tools:

- Kitchen scale
- Large mixing spoon
- Measuring cups and spoons
- Medium casserole dish
- Medium mixing bowl
- Sieve for dusting powdered sugar

Instructions:

1. Preheat the oven to 375°F.

2. Pour the frozen berries on the bottom of a medium casserole dish and add in the tapioca flour, the lemon juice, and 2 tablespoons of sugar. Toss to lightly coat the berries with the tapioca and sugar. Set aside.

3. In a medium mixing bowl, combine the remaining sugar, almond flour, potato starch, coconut flour, baking powder, and salt. Pour in the melted coconut oil, soy milk, and vanilla; mix well with a large spoon.

4. Dollop the cobbler dough on top of the berries—it doesn't have to cover all of the berries, just spread it out as best as you can.

5. Place the casserole dish in the oven and let the cobbler bake until golden brown and crisp on top, around 25–30 minutes.

6. Serve with a dusting of powdered sugar, and a dollop of plant-based yogurt or ice cream and enjoy!

From The Jewish Food Hero Kitchen

OLIVE OIL CHOCOLATE BROWNIES

Contributed by Debbie Stern

PREP TIME: 10 minutes | **COOK TIME:** Approx. 30 minutes
TOTAL TIME: 40 minutes | **YIELD:** 16 pieces

This recipe is my Mom's Passover brownie recipe that she made every year. Today, I host the Passover seder at my home, so now I am making these brownies: everyone in our extended family looks forward to eating them every Passover. I don't like coffee in general, but I like it in this recipe.

Ingredients:

- 2 eggs
- ¾ cup sugar
- ½ cup olive oil
- ¼ teaspoon salt
- ½ cup Passover cake meal (also called matzo meal)
- 60 grams (2 ounces) bitter chocolate (kosher for Passover Pareve), chopped
- 1 teaspoon instant coffee

Tools:

- Chopping board
- Kitchen scale
- Large mixing bowl
- Large spoon
- Measuring cups and spoons
- Microwave-safe bowl
- Pan, 8" x 8"
- Sharp knife
- Spatula
- Toothpick
- Whisk

Instructions:

1. Preheat the oven to 350°F / 180°C.
2. In a large bowl, whisk eggs and then add sugar. With a spatula, mix completely and then add oil, salt, and the Passover cake meal. Mix mixture until well mixed.
3. Place the chopped chocolate and instant coffee in a microwave bowl. Melt chocolate in the microwave for approximately 60 to 90 seconds, depending on your microwave.
4. Once the chocolate and coffee mixture is all melted, add it to the brownie mixture.
5. Blend everything and then pour mixture into a greased 8" x 8" pan.
6. Bake for about 20–30 minutes.
7. It is done when a toothpick comes out clean.

DEBBIE STERN has an agriculture degree in plant science. She loves trying different recipes and finding the best-tasting ones. She doesn't like packaged foods and prefers to make homemade food. She lives in Winnipeg with her husband and sons and extended family.

POMEGRANATE AND ROSE JELLY

Contributed by The Jewish Food Hero Kitchen

PREP TIME: 10 minutes, plus 1 hour chilling time | **COOK TIME:** 5 minutes
TOTAL TIME: 1 hour 15 minutes | **YIELD:** 20–25 jelly cubes

Remember Jell-O for American Passover seder dessert in the 1980s? This pomegranate and rose jelly comes together in no time and tastes like a fragrant trip to Jerusalem. The gelling agent we are using is agar agar which makes these jelly cubes vegan, but also means that the jelly will take a lot less time to set compared to jello set with gelatine. You can use this recipe as a template to play around with different jelly flavors—just replace the pomegranate juice with any juice of your choice and use different toppings—like green apple juice with chopped pistachios or blueberry juice with some grated lemon peel and poppy seeds.

Ingredients:

- 1 ½ cups pomegranate juice
- ½ cup water
- 2 tablespoons sugar
- 1 tablespoon rose water (optional)
- 1 ½ teaspoons agar agar powder
- 2 tablespoons rose petals

Tools:

- Glass dish or container to set the jello in
- Measuring cups and spoons
- Rubber spatula
- Sharp knife
- Small saucepan
- Whisk

Instructions:

1. Combine pomegranate juice, water, sugar, rose water, and agar agar in a small saucepan and bring to a boil over high heat, whisking often.
2. Once the mixture begins to boil, stir constantly with a whisk and allow to boil for a full 2 minutes. This will ensure the agar agar activates to make jello.
3. Pour the mixture into a glass dish or a container and sprinkle the rose petals on top of the jelly.
4. Allow to cool for 10 minutes at room temperature, then transfer to the fridge to fully set and cool for about 1 hour. Slice into squares and enjoy!

From The Jewish Food Hero Kitchen

SAGO GULA MELAKA:
SAGO PUDDING WITH PALM SUGAR

Contributed by Rosita E. Goldstein

PREP TIME: 10 minutes | **COOK TIME:** 35 minutes
TOTAL TIME: 45 minutes | **YIELD:** 8 ⅓-cup servings

"Sago Gula Melaka" is a dessert of sago pudding, served with gula melaka syrup and coconut milk. Gula melaka is also known as palm sugar, and you may substitute it with dark brown sugar. This is one of our family's favorites, and we often serve it to guests for Shabbat dinner dessert. It is best served cold.

This dish was first introduced to me in my formative years in Indonesia. Over time, I have modified the recipe. One of the reasons that sago gula melaka is so good is that—besides being deliciously inviting—it is also pareve, leaving me with the freedom to create my main course of either meat or dairy for my guests.

Ingredients:

For the sago:

- 1 liter water
- 200 grams round sago

For the gula melaka or brown sugar syrup:

- 200 grams of gula melaka
- 200 milliliters water
- 2 pandan leaves, tied into a knot
- Pinch of salt

Coconut milk sauce:

- 200 milliliters coconut milk
- 150 milliliters water
- 2 pandan leaves, tied into a knot

Tools:

- Kitchen scale
- Large bowl
- Measuring cups and spoons
- Saucepans x 3, one with a lid

- Small serving glasses or bowls
- Spatula
- Spoon
- Strainer

Instructions:

Make the sago:

1. In a pot, bring the water to a boil.
2. Add the sago and stir it a few times with a spoon to prevent the sago from sticking together. Cover the pot with a lid, turn down the flame, and simmer on a low heat for 15 minutes. Make sure you stir the sago every few minutes, especially the sides and the bottom of the pot, to prevent it from sticking.
3. After 15 minutes of simmering, the sago will turn partially translucent and you will see white dots. Turn off the flame and cover the pot with a lid. Let the sago continue cooking by itself for 8 minutes.
4. Pour the cooked sago into a big bowl of cool water and drain (repeat this process a few times), then set aside.

Make the gula melaka syrup:

5. Put all the syrup ingredients into a saucepan. Mix with a spatula and simmer on a medium-low heat for five minutes or until the gula melaka has dissolved.

6. Bring the syrup to a boil, then turn off the stove and set aside.

Make the coconut milk sauce:

7. Put all the coconut milk sauce ingredients into another saucepan and mix with a spatula, and simmer on medium-low heat until it boils, about 5 minutes. Turn off the heat and set aside.

Assemble the pudding:

8. Take small serving glasses or bowls. Pour ⅓ cup of cooked sago into each.

9. Pour 4 teaspoons of coconut milk on top of the cooked sago, then top them with 3 teaspoons of gula melaka syrup. You may add or reduce the coconut milk and gula melaka syrup to taste.

ROSITA E. GOLDSTEIN grew up in Jakarta, Indonesia, and now makes her home in Singapore with her husband Harvey and their four children. Rosita is passionate about her childhood Indonesian tastes and Jewish food. After years of being asked to share her recipes, Rosita published a cookbook *My Secret Recipes*. She shares her recipes on Facebook @Rosita'sFamilyHomeCooking.

TISHPISHTI: WALNUT CAKE SOAKED IN MILK WITH CARDAMOM, HONEY, AND RUM

Contributed by The Jewish Food Hero Kitchen

PREP TIME: 10 minutes, plus 1 hour 10 minutes chilling time
COOK TIME: 40–45 minutes
TOTAL TIME: 55 minutes, plus 1 hour 10 minutes chilling time | **YIELD:** 12 slices

Tishpishti is a Sephardic Jewish nut cake for Passover. Tishpishti is known for the sweet and comforting taste of baked apples, the buttery satisfying depth from walnuts, and a melt-in-your-mouth texture.

This version has some modern health upgrades. Using quinoa flour instead of matzo meal makes the cake lighter and higher in protein, not to mention better for our digestion. In place of refined sugar, honey gives a natural, rich, and multi-layered sweetness, and minimally processed coconut sugar has a lower glycemic index and contains vitamins and minerals.

This is a delicious cake for Passover and is also pleasing all year around.

Ingredients:

- 2 large eggs
- ½ cup coconut sugar (if you cannot find it, use regular white sugar)
- 2 apples, finely grated
- 1 cup unsweetened applesauce
- ½ cup coconut oil, melted
- 2 cups quinoa flour
- ½ cup walnuts, ground
- 2 teaspoons ground cinnamon
- ¼ teaspoon salt
- ½ cup walnuts, roughly chopped
- 1 cup unsweetened almond milk
- 4–5 cardamom pods
- 1 tablespoon orange zest
- 3 tablespoons honey
- ¼ cup rum (optional, replace with additional almond milk if not using)

Tools:

- Baking pan, 9" x 13"
- Grater
- Large bowl
- Measuring cups and spoons
- Small saucepan
- Spatula
- Whisk

Instructions:

1. Preheat the oven to 350°F and grease a 9" x 13" baking pan with some melted coconut oil.
2. In a large bowl, whisk the eggs with the sugar until combined. Add in the grated apples, applesauce, and coconut oil. Continue whisking until smooth.
3. Add in the quinoa flour, cinnamon, ground walnuts, and salt. Gently mix until the batter is smooth, then fold in the walnut pieces.
4. Transfer the batter into the prepared baking pan and bake until the cake becomes golden and starts pulling away from the sides, around 40–45 minutes.
5. While the cake bakes, add the milk, cardamom, and orange zest to a small saucepan and place over medium-low heat. Let the milk simmer gently for 15 minutes. Remove from the heat, discard the cardamom pods, and stir in the honey and rum.
6. Once the cake is done, allow it to cool for 10 minutes, then slice as desired, either in squares or in the traditional baklava-shaped pattern—but don't remove it from the pan yet.
7. Pour the warm milk mixture over the cake and let it soak for at least an hour.

From The Jewish Food Hero Kitchen

—— 🌿 ——

TWIX BARS: CHOCOLATE AND CARAMEL LAYERED SHORTBREAD

Contributed by Celeste Hackel

PREP TIME: 15 minutes, plus 1 hour chilling time | **COOK TIME:** 10 minutes
TOTAL TIME: 1 hour 25 minutes | **YIELD:** 10 twix bars

The Twix bar was invented in the United Kingdom in 1967 and later introduced to the United States in 1979. It is a popular chocolate bar with a biscuit base and caramel layer, all coated in milk chocolate. My homemade Twix recipe, inspired by the classic bar, is vegan and kosher-for-Passover! The shortbread layer blends almond and coconut flours with coconut oil, maple syrup, vanilla, and a pinch of salt. The dreamy caramel layer features almond butter, maple syrup, vanilla, and a touch of salt. And to top it off, a chocolate layer made with dark chocolate chips and a hint of coconut oil. Loved by all, this recipe is bound to become an annual Passover favorite that you'll make all year round!

Ingredients:

For the shortbread layer:
- 1 cup almond flour
- ¼ cup coconut flour
- ¼ cup coconut oil, melted and cooled
- 2 ½ tablespoons maple syrup
- ½ teaspoon vanilla
- Pinch salt

For the caramel layer:
- ⅔ cup runny natural almond butter
- ⅓ cup maple syrup
- 1 teaspoon vanilla
- Pinch salt

For the chocolate layer:
- ¾ cup dark chocolate chips
- 1 teaspoon coconut oil

For serving:
- Flaky salt (optional)

Tools:

- Loaf pan, 7" x 10" (18 x 25cm)
- Measuring cups and spoons
- Microwave-safe bowl
- Mixing bowls
- Mixing spoons
- Parchment paper
- Rubber spatula
- Sharp knife
- Small saucepan

Instructions:

---

1. Preheat the oven to 350°F / 180°C.
2. In a medium bowl, combine all the shortbread layer ingredients.
3. Press into a 7" x 10" loaf pan lined with parchment paper.
4. Bake for 10 minutes, then cool completely.
5. Next, make the caramel layer. Place almond butter, maple syrup, vanilla, and salt in a small saucepan over medium-low heat and mix to combine just until simmering, less than a minute.
6. Pour the caramel mix over the cooled shortbread layer crust and freeze to set for about 30 minutes.
7. When the caramel layer has set, melt the chocolate chips and oil in the microwave, stirring every 30 seconds until smooth.
8. Pour the melted chocolate over the caramel layer, tilting the pan to coat completely.
9. Refrigerate for approximately 20–30 minutes until set (you can leave them longer than this, but then the chocolate might crack while slicing).
10. Divide into 2 halves, then cut each half into five bars.
11. Sprinkle with flaky salt if desired and enjoy.

CELESTE HACKEL is a wife, busy mom, and health coach passionate about simple, nutritious, and delicious family-friendly recipes. Balancing it all inspired her mission to make healthy living low-stress and enjoyable. "Eat like you love yourself" is her mantra because we all deserve good food that's good for us. Explore her approachable, whole food recipes on Instagram @healthy.to.the.core.

ACKNOWLEDGEMENTS
AND FINAL NOTE

Thank you to all the contributors who generously shared their special recipes for this community collection.

Thank you to Turner Publishing for supporting this community cookbook, for responding to my questions and concerns throughout the project, and shepherding this project to publication.

To Bonny Coombe, another good time! You are shining and achieving with Lakhon Komnit ("thinking theater" in Khmer) in Cambodia, through your hard work and dedication!

Thank you to readers from the Jewish Food Hero Substack newsletter.

To my Mother and Father, for their unconditional love and support and instilling in me a love of candy and chocolate!

A Charles, merci de m'avoir appris par l'exemple que toute la nourriture doit être appréciée et savourée sans jamais être précipitée et le plaisir et la modération sont essentiels.

Yaël, eating a treat with you every day is a daily pleasure. New motto: K.Y.P.S.

Je t'aime.

GOING FORWARD

If I left out your favorite recipe, I am sorry. There are so many dessert recipes that could have been in this book, and I wish I could have included everyone's favorites.

Going forward I will be continuing my efforts to develop Jewish Food Hero. I would appreciate your help with this. Please send your suggestions and favorite recipes to my email, kenden@jewishfoodhero.com, so I can try to include them in a future project.

ABOUT THE AUTHOR

KENDEN ALFOND is a psychotherapist who began Jewish Food Hero because she was looking to connect with other Jewish people who care about healthy eating and modern Jewish life. She lives in Paris, France.

Kenden is also the author of:

- *Jewish Food Hero Cookbook*
- *Feeding Women of the Bible, Feeding Ourselves*
- *Beyond Chopped Liver: 59 Jewish Recipes Get a Vegan Health Makeover*
- *Feeding Women of the Talmud, Feeding Ourselves*
- *Kosher Macros: 63 Recipes for Eating Everything (Kosher) for Physical Health and Emotional Balance.*

Connect with The Jewish Food Hero:

https://jewishfoodhero.substack.com

INDEX

www.ingramcontent.com/pod-product-compliance
Lightning Source LLC
Chambersburg PA
CBHW061235150426
42812CB00055BA/2593